T0156793

Holy Sexuality

Beginning With Questions

Becky R. Patton

WESTBOW
PRESS
A DIVISION OF THOMAS NELSON

WestBow Press books may be ordered through booksellers or by contacting:

WestBow Press
A Division of Thomas Nelson
1663 Liberty Drive
Bloomington, IN 47403
www.westbowpress.com
1-(866) 928-1240

All the stories used in this book are used with permission. I have intentionally not used names in order to protect the privacy of each individual.

Unless otherwise indicated, Scripture quotations are from the New American Standard Bible (NASB) Copyright © 1960, 1962, 1963, 1968, 1971, 1972, 1973, 1975, 1977, 1995, by the Lockman Foundation, used with permission.

Front cover image: Kathryn Hanson Photography ©2010

Other Scripture references are from the following source:
The Message (MSG), © 1993. Used by permission of NavPress Publishing Group.

ISBN: 978-1-4497-0672-2 (sc)
ISBN: 978-1-4497-0671-5 (e)
Library of Congress Control Number: 2010939517
Printed in the United States of America
WestBow Press rev. date: 1/3/2014

Dedication

to my friend, mentor, and daddy ... you taught me to ask questions and encouraged me to keep asking. I miss you daily and hold the truest essence of you within.

Dick R. McCauley
1930–2006

Words of Thanks

Any bookstore houses a plethora of books. Behind every one is an author, but beyond that are uncountable others, whose voice of encouragement and challenge coaxed those words to life in book form.

As I've worked faithfully to bring forth the words and call God has given me, I see an intricately woven pattern of lives that have been brought together on my behalf. Together, they have helped me bring forth words and expand on them; each builds on the other, all belong together, and nothing is wasted.

With overwhelming gratitude, I acknowledge this symphony of voices, these saints—past and present—who have invested in my life. You know who you are, and your presence is represented in the new harmony of life carried within these words.

Thank you!

~becky

Contents

Some thoughts for you the reader.

A number of years ago, in the middle of the night, I was yanked from sleep by yet another troubling dream of being chased by a sexual attacker. As I stood by the window, looking at the night landscape, the moon reflected a shining path of light on top of the snow. It seemed to extend directly to me. As I intentionally held the unsettling dream, a simple prayer uttered from my lips: "Teach me to stand strong in my dreams … I don't want to run anymore."

I slipped on my robe and stepped out into the snow. The brutal cold burned my bare feet, but as I stood in spite of it, I could feel the warmth of my feet gradually melt the snow underneath me. When I stepped back into the house, the imprint of my feet lingered, and the light of the moon seemed to shift, shining on that very spot. Instead of being hidden by the darkness, my footprints were bathed in light.

Over the course of the months that followed, when the dreams would again threaten me, I fought to stand in a new way. I began to reclaim the "good" of my sexuality and stand against the "bad" that I had experienced. Truly healing from my past meant not running from it. What I once feared now became a part of my healing and transformation.

I am not a poet, theologian, or scientist, but I have found common threads in each that, when joined together, create deeper understanding of my own sexual journey. I am humbly aware of the words others invested in print that helped me find language and hope to explore the new ancient truths revealed in scripture. So, I write with intention to add my words to this sacred cycle.

I write because ...

- Women and men continue to ask ...
- There are so many unaddressed questions about sexuality ...
- I have tasted freedom and joy in my sexuality ...

I write knowing ...

- Words are inadequate to fully describe the wild gift of sexuality ...
- I will never be finished learning; my journey continues ...

I write for ...

- Hope to be stirred in seemingly hopeless places ...
- Churches to find language that is relevant ...
- The wounded spirit that is thirsty ...
- Single friends navigating a "quick-fix" culture ...

I write inspired by ...

- My husband's courage and wisdom ...
- My daughters, who value their God-designed femininity and strength ...
- My friends' continued sacrifice of time to help me share this message ...
- The generous hope and healing of God ...

The words you now hold began penning themselves in my dreams, conversations, and relationships years before there was ever a thought of putting them on paper. In fact, I never imagined writing a book. I have fought it, stalled out, and dismissed it as another's job—fully aware that there are others more qualified and more eloquent than I.

Words by themselves merely rest on a page, taking up space. It is our Creator who breathes life through words to create something new.

As you explore the topic of Holy Sexuality, you have the opportunity to recognize how something incredibly beautiful has unfortunately become incredibly distorted. Yet, a beautiful core is waiting to be remembered and rediscovered within every man and woman. Each person's journey is wholly their own, yet I know there are commonalities that we can all explore together. May these words provide you with both an opportunity to examine your own sexuality journey and some keys to what you are intended to experience.

It was the northern shores of Minnesota that provided me a wild and isolated space to gather together these words. I felt out of place in the woods, overwhelmed by the task, and an obvious foreigner in a land with no Internet access. The noise of the city was left behind, and the questions many had shared filled the quiet and began to propel me. I would do my very best to find language that could honor the original mysteries—both inspiring and holy—buried within our sexuality.

As encouragement for my writing getaway, a friend had given me a framed image of her daughter's innocent, cupped hands, extended as if offering a gift. By all appearances, the hands are empty and waiting to be filled. But, as I sat with the image, I realized the hands are filled with something more—her story.

Our dreams, longings, disappointments, and expectations can be gathered up and brought to God. It is by showing up and staying engaged that we make space for the power of God to access and transform each part of our journey. It is my prayer that these words trigger an awareness of your truest identity in God, that you find language for your questions, and that you discover the vibrations of creation that rest within you and your journey.

Tucked in the corner of this framed picture I now treasure is an invitation that I extend to you as well:

Bring what you have, and God will join you.

CHAPTER 1

Starting with Questions

Who questions much shall learn much, and retain much.
Francis Bacon

Just Beneath the Surface

We sat in a local coffee shop, catching up on life. She listened to me with curiosity and intent, sipping her tea, and our conversation moved to the intricacy of relationship struggles. I admired that even from the grandmother stage of life, she was intentionally learning to do relationships better. I trusted this strong and gentle woman and valued her words and actions. She had informally mentored me for years.

As I shared about my own recent relationship struggles, she responded with questions. With the precision of a surgeon, she skillfully cut and explored beneath the surface of my responses. Some of her questions I answered with ease; others caused me to pause. Certain questions pricked my pride and fear and made me want to flee. Instead, I quickly chuckled and ushered us to less-revealing ground, assuring her I was not struggling and suppressing what her words stirred within me.

Her questions unearthed hidden wounds and fiercely held assumptions about sexuality and sex. While my sexuality began the moment I was conceived, the choice to embrace and engage fully with my sexuality has been a lifelong journey. My mentor/friend's challenging questions continued to haunt me and ultimately became a marker on this long and winding path. There have been many key markers as I look back, but the real-life questions that held the greatest transformational power have come from the least expected sources and at the most unexpected times. Transformative truth is rarely convenient and has little respect for my timetable.

Stirring Questions

I was on Lake Superior, fishing for salmon, when I felt the faint movement of my first child within me. I froze in awe and wonder that this life was initiating movement. Simultaneous with my joy came a question from deep inside: "How am I going to protect this child?" Throughout the following months, despite my efforts to dismiss it, the life within repeatedly pushed this question to the surface.

As the life continued to stir throughout my pregnancy, old, troubling images began to surface as well—images that seemed vaguely familiar, frightening, and yet fuzzy.[1] Equally, a fierce desire to protect this life rose and demanded attention. I was suddenly feeling wedged between two worlds—one held the future and one held the past. I was caught in a past-future collision. How could I reconcile the two?

The truth was that as a young child, I had experienced sexual abuse. I knew the trauma of being overwhelmed by another and the helplessness of not having a voice. This precious new life within was triggering long-held fears that had rooted and lay undisturbed deep within me.

---

1   I would later learn that the brain allows us to store painful memories in ways that prevent us from even seeing them as pain. Like a misplaced computer file, a keyword search is needed to reveal its hidden place; while hidden, it is not erased.

As a child, I didn't have language to ask for help from my parents, fearing that I would somehow let them down. I sought to protect those who were my protectors. [2] I carefully hid my reality and acted out my pain through suppressed anger, random rebellion, and ultimately, sexual promiscuity. I ignored what I could not define until it became a faint recollection, stored in the attic of my brain and covered with dust ... seemingly forgotten and irrelevant. Slowly but surely, I mastered the act of segregating the past from the present.

Roots to Remember

I grew up in a traditional home in the 1960s. We moved frequently due to my father's job, and I learned quickly how to adapt and adjust to new things and leave old things behind.

My father was a pastor, so church and religion were foundational parts of my life. The Bible revealed the history of an interactive God, and heaven held future hope, but I was unable to see God as present in the here and now. I respected God but feared that a heavy gavel could drop at any minute from this judicial ruler.

For me, the church seemed to hold little relevance when it came to God and sex; the two didn't exist in the same time zone. God and sex? It was so unfathomable that the concept was not even on my radar screen.

The very nature of two coming together sexually is to surrender one's self physically and emotionally to another. This naked surrender and interchange holds the power to expose hidden, vulnerable emotions.

By the time I married, the past felt safely locked away. Sex within marriage held moments of ecstasy and joy but also an aching sensation; I often felt like little more than an object, invisible in the midst of sex. I desperately wanted my husband to value me, but I held little ability to value myself. When the pain of my past started

---

2   I am intentional about not sharing images here; others need not hold these images and memories. My abuse was sprinkled throughout my childhood at the hands of both men and women and ended in my early teen years.

to emerge, I would silence it quickly by falling into familiar patterns of anger and rebellion. Sex was such a loaded, confusing thing; was it really worth it?

Is sex even necessary for a marital relationship?

And if so, what is permissible?

I wanted guidance beyond what the magazines and cultural trends were offering, so I returned to the Bible of my youth and began to search the scriptures. I landed in Leviticus 15, which holds the laws of purification for the children of Israel. These rules are quite detailed, but they only raised more questions and left me more frustrated.[3]

Can I have sex when menstruating?[4]

Is sexual pleasure sin?

The laws of purification were written to teach Israel, a nation just freed from slavery, how to live. These principles were akin to a Health 101 class for people who, after living in oppression and slavery for hundreds of years, had no idea what was right or wrong, healthy or unhealthy.

Sexual interaction with another human forges a deep emotional connection; it carves a path and deposits remnants of another within us. The emotional scarring from my past was being revealed through sexual intercourse in the present. To ease the emerging pain, I used sex as a means of manipulation within my marriage—giving just enough to get what I wanted. As my journey and struggles continued, my questions were changing from "what's permissible?" to:

Will I ever enjoy sex without guilt, pain, or shame?

---

3   These are used as black-and-white rules for sex by some traditions, while other traditions use the same passage as proof of irrelevance regarding the Bible and sex.

4   There was a strong control motivation running through many of my questions at this point in my life.

How can something so pain-filled become good?

Why did God create sex?

Can pleasure be holy?

In my frustration, I sought out pastors I knew; in this case, all happened to be male. I was seeking spiritual guidance and ultimately wanted to know that God was real and had something relevant to add to my sexual quest. My questions elicited stunned silence in these pastors and could clear a room quicker than a fire drill. If I did receive a response, it was typically, "I'll get back to you"[5] or "Submit to your husband and everything will be fine."[6]

Believe me, this wasn't a terribly comfortable situation for me either! I turned the color of ripe eggplant when trying to speak about the topics that held such ache and frustration for me. My questions led people to avoid me at all costs. And because I asked, I got labeled "the one with the problem." I soon realized that no one knew how to answer my questions. I pushed sexuality and spirituality further apart, which only created more questions for me.

Is God ashamed of sex?

Does God turn away when we engage in sex?

I felt even more lost and confused—now by my faith community's silence, avoidance, and labeling.

Rooted to the Garden

The Bible clearly states that we are made in the image of God. In the words of J. Philip Newell, an author, theologian, and minister in the Church of Scotland, "At the heart of who we are is the love of God, the wisdom of God, the creativity, imagination and wildness

---

5   No one ever did get back to me.
6   Herein lies one of the deepest challenges facing the church: the opportunity to educate men and women about their bodies in a way that empowers them in the art of *making love* within marriage.

of God … God is not present 'beside' the human merely, but *in* the human."[7]

Engaging in sexual intercourse with my husband was exposing the very core of my being, created in the image of God. My sexuality could not be separated from my spirituality. The very root of sexuality and spirituality were woven together from within God's original design of man and woman.

The deepest roots within me yearned for the Garden, when I was crafted in the image of God. So, who better to teach me about this mysterious interconnection than the One who created it?

I walked through an art show recently and was drawn to an intriguing photograph. The creator of this piece stood nearby, and I asked a simple question, "What prompted you to shoot this photo?" She explained how she created the image, inviting me into the intricacies of seeing, holding, and ultimately capturing it with her camera. Her words lent an alluring sense of calm and peace to the image. I saw and understood more because I sought her perspective; I experienced more because she engaged with me and invited me into the fuller story of her creative work.

Our natural curiosity is meant to be a connection point to God. God longs to reveal greater depths in what has been created and invites us to see a fuller story from the Creator's vantage point. Our curiosity about sexuality is *good* and *God ordained*. Our questions are an opportunity to expand our relationship with God and our understanding of how we mysteriously bear God's image within.

I am reminded of a cold winter's night when I stumbled into my newborn's room to feed her. We hadn't yet hung the drapes, so the moonlight was spilling over and around us as I nursed her in the rocking chair. As I gazed down at her eager, sweet face, I heard yet another provocative question: Will you feed her from love or hate?

7   Newell, J. Philip. *The Book of Creation: an Introduction to Celtic Spirituality.* New York: Paulist Press, 1999. 84. Print

It was as if God was speaking right to me.

I loved this child desperately and immediately recognized that the milk serving as her life force was tainted with a subtle, hidden hatred that I felt for myself as a woman and as a sexual being.

I was in awe that God would visit me in this way and reveal that I didn't value myself as part of what had been created. As I crawled back into bed, I cried and prayed a simple prayer: "God, I don't know what it would look like or how it can change, but please help me love this body you have given me."

God Isn't Scared of Our Questions

I find questions woven into every book of the Bible, Old and New Testament. Jesus masterfully models ease with questions as a natural part of dialogue and interaction with others. Instead of inhibiting or prohibiting curiosity from certain cultural places, Jesus makes space for questions in the middle of synagogues, while conversing over a meal, when roused from sleep, when taking a walk. Jesus seems very intentional about honoring questions, while at the same time, tracing back to the motive or source of the question. In response, He poses a counterquestion, extends a hand to heal, or allows a pregnant silence that reveals one's heart. But, never does Jesus belittle the person or the question.

I once worked with a woman who challenged my view of God with this simple sentence, "Becky, I don't think God is quivering with fear that you are asking a question. I think He is jumping up and down and saying, 'Pick me! Pick me! I want to show you something.'"

Over time, I've come to realize that questions reveal the inner landscape of our thought life. Questions channeled toward God are like battery cables connected from a drained battery to the original source: when properly connected, they channel a charge that can return what was lifeless and dead back to life.

A Manner of Silence

While eating dinner and discussing the topic of sex with some friends one night, I noticed that each time our male friend said the word "sex," he would adjust his glasses, lean in, and whisper. As the night continued, I found myself becoming more agitated. His discomfort fed my own discomfort. It was as if we were violating some secret code, and I wondered, *Why is it so uncomfortable for us to talk about sex?*

Is it shame about our own sexuality that leads us to revert to such junior high behavior as whispers and speculation? We lower our voices and speak in hushed tones about sexuality as if it were a dreaded distant relative who had shown up without invitation. Do we think God is embarrassed of—or even has disdain for—our sexuality and sexual design?

Our silence as a church community on the topic of sexuality and sex creates more questions. It leads to dangerous misinformation and assumptions by driving people to the Internet, magazines, videos, and locker rooms for some kind of help on this complex and intimate subject. Our culture tutors us—from its painfully limited understanding of God, its benevolent, intentional Creator.

Places of not knowing are places of vulnerability and, many times, places of great risk. Perhaps that's why religion and the church tend to view questions as needing a quick answer. As a result, prepackaged, tidy, seemingly relevant answers squelch the potential of what a question can unfold and reveal. In the poignant words of Henri Nouwen, "Answers without questions damage the soul."[8]

The process of dealing with questions is vulnerable and challenging for all of us—individuals and institutions alike. Yet, within each question lies the potential of being stretched, opened, and transformed by something new.

---

8   To the best of my knowledge, the original source of this quote is Fr. Henri J. M. Nouwen. Confirmation is pending. For more information on his writings, please visit www.henrinouwen.org.

Questions Unfold Mystery

While on vacation some years back, I was contemplating my damaged view of sexuality and seeking to discover the essence of God's image within me. I found myself sitting on a rock in the middle of a raging Colorado stream.[9] I had jumped out onto this rock alone, only to find that there was not enough surface space to launch myself back to shore. I was trapped. With the roar of the water in my ears, I lay in the center to let the water rush around me. I felt the dull familiar ache return within me, and I asked God when it would all be *finished*. Or would I forever be stuck in this place?

From deep within, I felt a question arise, "Can you place your foot in the same waters twice?" I looked at the rushing water and realized that the very moment I gazed at one spot, it was no longer there—it continued to move. God was moving me in and through, reclaiming and restoring my truest identity as a woman. No, I would not reside in this place of pain forever, but it was a part of the journey to greater freedom.

One morning a few years later, I woke with a deep sense of gratitude and joy, reflecting on intimate moments with my husband. Yet, there was something deeper still, calling me to remember. Suddenly, I was hearkened back to Colorado and felt the heat of the rock on my back, the roar of water in my ears, and the presence of that moment years before. God was reminding me that the waters of pain had not held me. The past, present, and future are a part of the moving water of God.

Questions can lead us to discover more—if we give them space and allow them to expand our thinking rather than redirect them to quick, easy answers. The very nature of God is to unfold and reveal the *ancient harmony* of truth, allowing us to discover and return to the ways we bear the image of God.

---

9   For me, the mountains of Colorado have consistently been a place of experiencing God's strength. With love and joy, I often say that God resides in Colorado and visits everywhere else.

Learning to Ask Questions

In this book, I am addressing the consistent questions I hear over and over again as I invite questions in the classes I teach. It is by no means an exhaustive list, but here are questions I hear most frequently:

- What does my sexuality have to do with my spirituality and God?
- Are men and women really that different, and why does it matter?
- What does singleness have to do with sexuality?
- If everyone is having sex, why wait until marriage?
- Is masturbation a sin?

As we embark on our journey into these questions, I hope you will notice your own personal questions stirring and allow them to rise to the surface. There are no formulas, no exact steps, and no easy answers. But, there is the opportunity to be awakened and transformed by God.

Let the questions serve as a guide on this spiritual quest to explore the mysterious roots of sexuality and spirituality's interwoven beginnings.

My own story continues, as I discover ever more about the beauty of my crafting as a sexual being. I share glimpses into my own journey only as a means of offering encouragement. There is a tendency in religious realms to turn one person's journey into a cookie-cutter, one-size-fits-all approach. Please don't read this book and try to travel the precise road I have walked. Instead, find the signposts within these words that help you recognize God calling you to continue on your own intimate, personal journey. I have absolutely no doubt in my mind that God has unique, creative ways for you to experience the transformation of your own sexuality.

Together, let's see what the questions have to teach us.

A "Quest" in Every "Question"

A quest makes me think of something to be learned, something noble, something mysterious out there just waiting to be discovered.

I am often invited into intimate questions that reflect personal struggles and deep confusion, but each holds potential for intimate discovery:

- She approached me with bright eyes and a pointed finger. "Where were you when I was getting married?" When I asked how long she had been married, she said forty-two years. Being in my forties, the straightforward answer was easy, but as I paused to be present, her deeper question poured forth: "Do you think I can experience some of this?"

- She sat at the back of the classroom, staring down at her desk. Her face was stoic, and there was no indication she was connecting with anything I was saying. After I left the classroom, we bumped into each other in the hallway. I asked her if she had anything she wanted to talk about from the morning session. She lowered her head, her shoulders began to shake, and gentle sobs began to escape from within. She had grown up being sexually abused and had buried it deep inside and hidden within a fortress of denial. Yet, her body was beginning to betray her in the form of extreme hives and anxiety attacks. "My body knows the truth, but I am scared; am I damaged beyond God's ability to heal?"

- I saw him standing off to the side, waiting, twisting the papers he held into a tight cone. He walked toward the door as if to leave and then returned, though making no sign of moving toward me. I gathered my computer, books, and papers and asked if he might help me carry them to my car. Although we casually conversed about the topic I had just taught, the words between us seemed empty. He placed my bag into the trunk of my car, and when he lifted his eyes to meet mine, the real questions came cascading out: "I would have made different choices ... why didn't someone tell me this earlier?"

- She said she was getting ready to celebrate her fiftieth wedding anniversary, and I congratulated her on navigating the joys and struggles of marriage. I asked her what she was going to do to celebrate, and she responded, "I am going to rediscover myself as a sexual being and ask my husband to forgive me for not valuing him sexually. I wish I could have heard these things years ago. Do you think I am too late?"

- She sat with resigned hopelessness in the chair, her fingers clinging to the shirt that covered her wrists and her recent physical release of the pain. I knew little of her story but could see the resulting pain in her eyes. She talked of being "used up" by sex and having nothing to look forward to, nothing she could offer within marriage. We talked of sex, pain, and the shadows that were haunting her from the partners that were too numerous to name or count. "What is the big deal about sex? "Will I ever experience anything good sexually?"

- He was successful in business and held the respect of his community but wrestled with sexual compulsions that left him exhausted and confused. He took the risk, broke the silence, and said, "No wonder I have been so frustrated. I thought God made sex as a test that I continually failed. Why aren't we taught about sex in this way?"

I continue to be awed by the sacred questions that are finally uttered, raw, real, long-buried questions that reveal a desire to discover something more. Pain-filled confusion is consistent across the questions I hear around this often-taboo topic of sex and sexuality. We've made assumptions, formed theories, and adjusted our expectations accordingly. Yet, the greatest discovery in this quest is God's abundantly generous nature to heal and set free.

While the world is seeking answers, it might seem strange to write a book on questions; yet, it seems to me the perfect place to begin.

PRAYER

God, as I venture into this new area of exploration, I simply ask that you would:

help me identify the core questions I carry …
challenge me to let go of any limiting assumptions …
expand my capacity to hold the questions as I look to you …

That I would have eyes to see you within my sexuality and to see my sexuality rooted deeply within you.

Amen

Some Questions for Reflection

- What has been more valued in your experience—questions or answers? How has this impacted your view of God?
- Have you held unanswered questions about your sexuality and/or sex? What are they?
- Is there anything vulnerable or challenging for you as you consider inviting God to meet you in your questions about sexuality?

CHAPTER 2

No Quick, Easy Answers

For an old idea to die and a new and better idea to take place, we
have to go through periods of confusion.
It is uncomfortable, sometimes painful ...
Nonetheless it is blessed because when we are in them,
we are open to the new, we are looking, we are growing.
Scott Peck
Further Along the Road Less Traveled

As We Embark on Our Quest: Chocolate as Metaphor

John Scotus Eriugena, a ninth-century Irish theologian and
Greek scholar, asserts that, "Everything which is true is totally
indestructible."[10] Anytime something confronts us or disrupts our
established way of thinking, there is a choice to make: whether to
drive the stake of our conviction deeper into the ground *or* listen
with ears of discernment to see if there is something there to learn.

It was while I was in London, passing by a beautiful display case
of chocolates from around the world, that a French chocolatier
confronted my deeply held dislike of chocolate. He simply asked me,
"Would you like to sample the chocolate?"

---

10   Eriugena, Johannes Scotus. *Periphyseon: Division of Nature,* Bellarmin, 1987.
      919A. Print.

My flat-out response was that I didn't like chocolate. Working for a U.S. based chocolate company for two years, with the fresh aroma greeting me each morning, had only solidified my deep disgust of this innocent bean. In fact, I'd developed elaborate schemes for ridding the chocolate coating from Heath and Snickers bars' wonderful insides. I had a forty-year track record of an unquestioning dislike of chocolate.

"No one who has *experienced* real chocolate could ever hate it," he asserted. "Would you explore chocolate with me?"

Instead of judging me or simply letting another American just pass him by, he began to engage me in a discussion. He asked questions about my experiences and my understanding and assumptions of chocolate. And this master chocolatier helped change my attitudes. He told me to do the following:

- Close your eyes.
- Let the chocolate linger on your tongue.
- Let it speak to you.

By accepting his invitation, my experience with chocolate dramatically changed and my long-held assumptions were transformed, but only when I experienced *real* chocolate.[11] I had to trust one who, through a different perspective, could see something that I could not see. He took me on a journey toward something authentic. Thanks to him, I now have one shelf in my freezer devoted to *very good* chocolate.[12]

Faulty Assumptions and Foundational Beliefs

Faulty assumptions are often difficult to recognize, unless we risk asking and allowing the disturbing questions to linger in our mind. It was the authentic chocolate that taught me what I really disliked was the sweetness that masked the truest taste of chocolate. If we are going to examine our foundations, we must recognize the places that we need to linger and allow the truth to speak to us.

---

11   Most American chocolate I had consumed contained more sugar than cocoa.
12   Best chocolate I have ever tasted? B. T. McElrath, Salty Dog!

As we explore the questions that follow, most of us will recognize faulty assumptions and lies that have crept into our thinking to form faulty beliefs and patterns of responding to all things sexual. For us to recognize our own assumptions, we will need to pause, wonder, and examine in a deeper way our own thinking regarding our views:

- Of sexuality
- Of ourselves
- Of God

What causes faulty assumptions?

Much of our view of sexuality is etched into our memories by experiences we had as children and young adults. There are three primary sources that inform and feed our sexuality:

Family of Origin Influence

Cultural Influence   Religious Influence

Our *family of origin* is where we first learn about sexuality/sex and acquire sexual language. We learn how to survive and navigate life from within the family system. While there is no perfect family, it is safe to say that we all have received, to varying degrees, some truths and misconceptions about our sexuality. As we recognize what we learned in our family—either directly or indirectly—we can choose what we want to carry forward and where we want to forge a new path.

Cultural influence comes through the media: music, movies, TV, magazines, and so on; social mores/trends; and arenas like politics. Traditionally, there have been pendulum swings from conservative to liberal sensibilities and back again in our culture. We tend to create cultural camps around what we believe and often surround ourselves with people who are like-minded and help reinforce our established attitudes.

There is also significant *religious influence* when it comes to our sexuality. Religious beliefs have had the greatest influence on culture and families for the longest period. Our religious beliefs from within church/synagogue/temple cultures have profound impact on our view of genders (roles, abilities, etc.) and of sexual behavior. Religion often perpetuates an elevated view of sexual sin. From abortion protests to heated banter on homosexuality, there seems a need to identify the poster child for "worst sin." Whether intentional or not, this has contributed to guilt and shame around sexual issues and even legitimate sexual questions. In fact, the last place many would choose to bring their questions, wonderings, and wounds would be to the church.

Upon what messages—explicit or implicit—have we built our beliefs of sexuality?

In seeking to find answers, we often innocently create barriers to define the lines that cannot be crossed physically. We craft encampments around the edges of these lines, holding to a definition rather than examining how or why we hold so tightly to this belief.

There can be discomfort in reexamining our deeply ingrained beliefs. Many of us would prefer a neat, tidy, well-established line that governs our assumptions, beliefs, and behaviors. Many would prefer the lack of a line as license and self-justification in charting their own self-defined courses. But, what if instead of ill-formed, black-and-white formulas, God wants to engage with us and help guide us to greater truth and greater freedom?

What if the "line" is more of an arrow leading to the heart of God?

Reexamining Our Foundational View of Sexuality

When most of us hear the word "sexuality," we immediately think of sex. Walk past any magazine or newsstand, and you will be inundated with the world's view of sexuality, which seems to be, "It's all about sex and seduction."

But sexuality is much, much more than just a physical engagement of the body. Sexuality is who we are as men and women. It is the unique lens—spirit, mind, and body—through which we view, perceive, and interact with God and others. It is about being fully alive to how we experience the world through our senses.

In fact, note the important distinctions in these words:

- *Seduce*—"to lead astray; corrupt; to draw away, as from principles"[13]
- *Sensuous*—"perceived by or affecting the senses; readily affected"[14]

The master chocolatier asked me to close my eyes and said, "Instead of thinking of this piece of chocolate as something to consume, slow down and feel it melting on your tongue." I fought my urge to hurry and stilled myself. With eyes closed, I let a small portion of truffle linger on my tongue.

To let something linger means to dwell with and spend time with it. Our senses are designed to awaken us to the fullness of being alive as sexual beings.

What have we assimilated that informs our definition of sexuality?

Innocence revealed

One hot summer day, my four-year-old daughter and a friend's son were eating Popsicles on the back deck. Their faces and arms were streaked with sticky orange residue. I went indoors to get a washcloth to clean them up, but when I returned, I found two children running

---

13   *Online Dictionary*. www.dictionary.com.
14   *Online Dictionary*. www.dictionary.com.

through the sprinkler. They dashed in and out of the water, laughing with utter abandon—completely naked and without any shame.

It was while watching this beautiful display of freedom that I realized innocence had been robbed from me. I had experienced sexual abuse, and many of my foundational beliefs about sexuality were born out of the resulting lies and shame. I was left with physical and emotional baggage and negative views about my own sexuality and about sex itself.

My life experiences had established patterns of thinking—brain patterns—that my body also embraced as truth:

- *Sex is wrong*—Because of how I first experienced sex, the beauty and sacredness of this act was stripped from me. There instead was an inherent dirtiness and darkness around sexual acts.
- *Sexuality is secret and shameful*—Make no mistake, silence speaks volumes. As a child, I did not have healthy language for my physical body. And within my faith community, there was certainly no acknowledgment of sexuality, which I interpreted as God wanting nothing to do with my physical body.

As I've talked with men about what shaped their views of sexuality, it's clear that very different perspectives can govern or fight for their thinking:

- *Sex is primarily about pleasure*—Because of how visual and accessible males genitals are, there is immediate evidence of the pleasurable sensations boys and men experience. This "pleasure principle" can easily take on a life of its own and quite literally shape views of sexuality.
- *Sex defines masculinity*—Locker room talk and beyond often focuses on conquest and measuring oneself accordingly as a man. Questions like, "Did you get some?" or, "How many corks have you popped?" serve

as a measure of masculinity. Having sex can serve as a trophy.

What messages have you unknowingly absorbed about your sexuality?

No matter what we have experienced and/or believed, it is only a part of the who we are. Our past—even if pain filled—does not dictate our sexual future. Looking back, I can see it: despite the pain I had internalized, something deeper still—the mark of God within me—knew something wasn't right. My spirit was literally fighting for the truth of my sexuality, a longing was held deep within, until it could safely emerge.

"The failures of our lives and the falseness of what we have become do not have the power to undo what God has woven into the very fabric of our nature."[15]

What is *your* foundational view of sexuality and how did you come to it?

Reexamining Our Foundational View of Self

Jesus called us to love God, and to love our neighbors as ourselves. But this often-referenced verse is rarely understood in its fullness.

> "Love the Lord your God with all your passion and prayer and intelligence. This is the most important, the first on any list. But there is a second to set alongside it: *Love others as well as you love yourself.* These two commandments are pegs; everything in God's Law and the Prophets hangs from them."[16]

Does our ability to love others really hinge on how well we love ourselves?

---

15   Newell, J. Philip. *The Book of Creation: an Introduction to Celtic Spirituality.* New York: Paulist Press, 1999. 86. Print.

16   Matthew 22: 37–39. *The Message*, emphasis mine.

Are there assumptions that cloud our view to the true beauty of who we are?

My children loved author A. A. Milne's tales of Winnie the Pooh. As a family, we read these stories over and over, quoted Pooh wisdom, and played in imaginary Hundred Acre Woods. One night, while I acted out Eeorye's commentary on why no one should listen to him because he amounted to nothing special, I recognized his words as my own.

I "loved" others. I reached out to the needy and lent a helping hand to my family, friends, and neighbors; this was a core part of how I lived life. But did my gestures convey the *purest* essence of love if I didn't love myself?

Can we truly love how God has made us—spirit, mind, and body? Do we find our true value and identity in being loved by God?

It has been challenging to learn to love myself. It is an ongoing, intentional choice to love this body of mine, to love the mind I have been given; and the choice—at times—is still challenging. But Jesus' words invite, encourage, and remind me. And as I let God's love fill me and deepen my love for myself, it somehow deepens my love for others as well. Created as a woman, I am a sexual being, and how I embrace that will determine how I live in this world.

Might this be the mysterious reality of Jesus' words to love others *as well as* we love ourselves?

Reexamining Our Foundational View of God

In my quest to understand my sexuality, I realized I had some very disordered assumptions about God:

- God only cares about my spirit—not my body.
- God didn't design my physical desires; they're a result of "the fall."
- God designed sex only for making babies.

As a woman, the messages I picked up from my faith community were that "my flesh" was bad, it was a woman's responsibility to make sure men were not led into temptation, and that God's stance on sex was little more than "No! Danger! Don't go there!" Couple this with "just do it" messages from our culture, and I assumed:

- Desire = sin
- Sex = shame
- Sexy = slutty

For me, God became little more than a distant party pooper, wanting to keep boys and girls, men and women from "real fun." God's views seemed unrealistic and out of touch with the pleasures of sex. I came to imagine a sneaky miser, dangling physical desire in front of me and waiting for me to fail.

But what I've learned cast a glaring light of truth on my ill-formed assumptions. Did you know the following:

- There are parts of our body God designed *intentionally for*—and in some cases *purely for*—pleasure.
- By digging into scripture's original text, there are fresh, timely, God-given insights into our sexuality that can otherwise be all-too-easily glossed over.
- God definitely designed men and women in unique ways—science is proving it—but rather than segregating us, those differences enrich family, business, and relationship settings when valued and partnered together.

This quest has totally revamped my view of God as one who not only created pleasure but intended that pleasure enrich and expand our relationship with the Creator.

Why no quick, easy answers?

I realize that most of us would love—and maybe even expect—a very clear list of answers and how-tos when it comes to our sexuality. Believe me, I can empathize; I spent more money than I care to think about on books, tapes,[17] and seminars, trying to find the quick, concise answers that would make me comfortable, address my fears, and heal my pain.

I find scripture very illuminating in that Jesus heals numerous people struggling with blindness, but never in the same way; instead, there are a variety of approaches—dirt, spit, water, touch, and words. There is only one commonality for all who were healed: *those seeking hope and healing came, and Jesus healed them.*

In this quest around our sexuality, God longs to meet and partner with each of us in unique ways. An overarching desire is for an intimate relationship with us.

Make no mistake: reviewing and examining long-established ways of thinking and responding is work. There will be no quick fix when it comes to our sexuality. But, the truest gifts come through the work of discovery. I believe that the journey of unfolding our sexuality can teach us about who we are and who God is within us. It is an invitation into a deeper relationship, an intimate unveiling that reveals an unimaginably wild and beautiful part of God.

Will you join me in reexamining your own assumptions as we walk together through the following chapters?

---

17   Prior to CDs or the Internet.

Some Questions for Reflection

- In what way was sexual awareness "awakened" within you?
- What is your foundational view of yourself as a sexual being? What has influenced or shaped this view?
- What has informed how you view your own body?
- What are the foundational views that you carry about who God is and how God views sexuality?

CHAPTER 3

Sexuality and Spirituality

One dwells with God by being faithful to one's nature.
One crosses God by trying to be something one is not.
Parker J. Palmer

Question #1:

What does sexuality have to do with spirituality?

Embracing Our Sexuality as Part of Our Design

Traditionally, the church has portrayed sexual desire as a wild demon that must be denied and/or squelched at all costs. Our culture, on the other hand, would say that sexual desire can't be controlled, can't be tamed.

Here's what many of us hear as the perspectives of our culture and the church:

Cultural View of Sexuality	Church's View of Sexuality
• Sexual drive can't be controlled • It's about pleasure • Deny the spirit • "Feels good = do it" • Freedom-no limitations	• Sexual drive must be squelched • It's about procreation • "Deny the flesh" • "Feels good" = Sin • All about limitations

The sad result is that we then end up living in a very polarized reality. The church would have us deny our physical desires. The culture would have us deny the spiritual/emotional realities of sex. To wonder if/how our sexuality and spirituality are intertwined requires that we address some foundational views of ourselves and of God:

- Is sexuality as a part of "our flesh" inherently sinful?
- Was God singularly focused on procreation when designing sex?
- Can sexual desire be both wild and good?

Is sexuality as a part of "our flesh" inherently sinful?

It really matters how we view the essence of who we are as men and women. It is vital that we embrace our physical and spiritual beings as rooted in the image of a God who is holy.

It is often said that we humans are sinful by nature. But, could it be that sin drives us away from recognizing and embracing what is our *true nature*: the image of God within us?

In the beginning God created ...[18]

"In the beginning," God created man and woman. The memory may be faint within all of us, but we are a part of this story, because we

---

18   Genesis 1:1.

all bear His image.[19] Man and woman—humankind—were created in the image of God.

Could we choose to listen in a new way to this old passage?

From the time I was a small child, I heard the story of creation and saw it acted out in pageant form or flannelgraph displays. Even as an innocent four-year-old girl, I experienced the drama and emotion of the story not in its miraculous creativity and beautiful display but in the dramatic letdown. The primary point of the story seemed to be this: the woman sinned and enticed the man to join her, and God sent them out of the Garden. What had been declared, "very good,"[20] suddenly became extremely and completely bad. The core question I was left with as a little girl was, do you think God was sad He made us?

As an adult, my questions turned elsewhere, and I began to wonder if there are other things this creation story had to say to us:

Was woman a part of God's original plan?

Was man a part of how woman was designed?

Did woman have a place in the creation story?

In an effort to keep things simple, had key elements of this story been sidelined? Are there others things God wants to say through the creation?

From the beginning of time, humankind was embedded with the image of God. "The God whom I know dwells quietly in the root system of the very nature of things."[21] In a real but mysterious way, each of us is rooted and grounded in who God is.

When our oldest daughter was a month old, a male friend who was holding her gently kissed her head and said to my husband, "It's a

---

19   Genesis 1:26, 27.
20   Genesis 1:31.
21   Palmer, Parker J. *Let Your Life Speak: Listening for the Voice of Vocation.* San Francisco: Jossey-Bass, 2000. 51. Print.

little creepy kissing her when she looks so much like you, but she's so beautiful I can't help myself." This baby girl bore the image of her earthly father. But, I believe that deeper still, it was the imprint of her Creator that drew our friend's heart to reach out and kiss her sweet head.

We were not created from nothing. We were created from the very essence of God. We exist only because God exists at the very core of who we are. If we remove the truest essence from us, we would cease to exist.

Alexander John Scott, a nineteenth century Scottish Chaplain, compares the fact that we bear God's image to the construction of royal garments of the era. The cloth used for making these garments had a single golden thread interwoven throughout; if the golden thread was removed, the very fabric unraveled.[22] The single golden thread was at the core, holding all elements together.

Many religious traditions have seemingly rushed to a quick, concise conclusion in response to the creation story's rendition of the man and the woman eating from the Tree of Knowledge of Good and Evil. We have been led to believe that at this turning point, humans lost the image of God, and the mark of sin became their true identity. But sin does not have the power to erase our Creator's fingerprints. At the core and the very essence of our being, humankind bears the image of God; sin clouds our vision, causing us to believe only what our eyes can see and not what our heart knows.

Grace restores our memory; it reboots our mental computer with the original software that integrates God's love into the very fiber of our being—spiritually, emotionally, and physically. John Scotus Eriugena speaks of, "the medicine of Divine Grace,"[23] an outpouring of God's abundant love in sending Jesus to shed real blood so that

22 Scott, A. J. *The Social Systems of the Present Day, Compared with Christianity: In Five Lectures.* London: Published at "The Pulpit" Office, by Sherwood, Gilbert and Piper, 1841. p. 348. Print.
23 Eriugena, Johannes Scotus. *Periphyseon:Division of Nature,* Bellarmin, 1987. p.872A-872B. Print.

we can see and touch our true identity and heal our deep infections. Jesus is the antidote for what has blinded our eyes to seeing that our true identity bears the image of God.

Regardless of my children's choices—good or bad—they will always bear the image of my husband and me, their parents. Their choices can separate them from us in a variety of ways, but there is no choice that can erase the foundational essence of who they are and what they carry within from us.

Deeper still, it is God's identity that is embedded within us.

So, where does sex fit into this created-in-God's-image equation?

God's Design for Sex: Procreation and/or Pleasure?

It seems laughable now, but for much of my life, I kept God separate from my sexuality and most definitely out of my bedroom. I'd come to understand my physical body as "fleshly," embarrassing, and unholy. I'd somehow managed to overlook the fact that God literally designed my physical body and actually enjoys the design of our bodies.

If we truly believe that God designed our physical bodies, there is purpose in examining the intricacy and intention of how the image of God is revealed in our bodies.[24] Physically, there are major revelations of who we are by how the image rests within our body's design. Can we dare to look for a Creator's signature and practical intentions for us in our physical bodies?

God designed us with the gift of five senses—seeing, smelling, hearing, touching, tasting—with which to experience the world around us. These faculties help alert us to dangerous situations by smelling a fire, seeing a car accident ahead, hearing a blood-curdling scream, and so on. But, our senses also allow us to experience beauty, delight, and pleasure in the world around us: seeing an awe-inspiring sunset, hearing a moving song, feeling a friend's warm hug. Senses

---

24   Genesis 1:27. More later, I promise!

and pleasure are an intentional part of God's design. To experience the beauty of the world around us is to experience more fully the God who created it all.

Do we believe God wants us to enjoy the pleasures that were created?

As a teenager, there was one year I unexpectedly stayed an extra week at summer camp. I ended up spending the weekend with the counselors and got to partake in their rejuvenating weekend activities. As I repeatedly slid down a waterfall, lay in the warm sun, and hung out with the counselors, I remember experiencing a deep pleasure and joy. As we were gathering our things to leave, a young woman commented, "This feels so good, it must be sin."

Have we inadvertently equated pleasure as bad? Is pleasure merely an accidental by-product beyond God's original intention?

Consider that there are aspects of our physical design that speak very clearly to God's desire that we experience pleasure:

For Men—The penis was certainly designed with vital functionality for the elimination of waste and impregnating a woman. But, the penis is also packed with nerve endings that transport powerful sensations to every part of a man's body, including his brain. Most men experience the sensory aspects of their penis as very good. Could God have designed the penis without this sensory gift? Absolutely, but God didn't. Instead, God created the man's penis as both highly functional and highly pleasurable.

For Women—The clitoris could be considered the genital counterpart to a man's penis, though it is distinctly different in its functionality. This intricate part of a woman's body is tucked inside her genital region, hidden from view and often overlooked. Yet, it has fourteen parts with even more nerve endings than the underside shaft of the penis! The clitoris's nerve endings connect with the brain and elicit sensations throughout the body; but, unlike the penis, it has no physical function in the body other than *to provide pleasure.*

Did God not know this when crafting the woman? Would we really believe that this mysterious, intricate, and complicated part of a woman was created by accident?

From the very beginning, God designed our physical bodies to experience pleasure. In fact, pleasure was designed as a way for us to connect with God—whether through a sunset; a musical score; a piece of art or a holy, physical connection with another human being.

I believe that God's deepest desire would be for us to experience the fullness of God by experiencing the fullness of *all* creation. As the creator of pleasure, God is seeking to reveal the deepest stores of abundance. Genesis reveals a longing for us to experience God rather than just to know about God. There is an eagerness to show humankind more of who we are through how we interact and engage with one another.

To be spiritually engaged with and fully alive to our sexuality is to be open to God and the world around us in a new way.

I have heard it said that the true character of a man is known by his actions as much as his words. Wouldn't this also be true of God? Don't we have to wonder about the view we have of God when we examine the intricate design of men and women's bodies in relation to our sexuality?

What kind of power and pleasure might sexuality have if it were partnered with the hand of the One who created it?

Wild but Good: An invitation to Live in the Tension

But how can something intended as beautiful hold so much pain for so many?

The prophet Ezekiel says that to be born of Eden is to be, "perfect in beauty and full of wisdom,"[25] but this does not mean we turn a blind

---

25 Ezekial 28:12.

eye to sin and the distortions it creates within our lives. J. Philip Newell explains sin's distortions and their consequences this way:

> Forgetful of who we are, we live out of ignorance instead of wisdom, fear instead of love, and fantasy instead of reality … The less we make use of the spiritual resources implanted at the heart of our being the more we come to believe they are not there. And the less we believe that such riches are within us the more we treat ourselves and another with a lack of respect.[26]

Statistics paint a dismal picture of the reality of pain and struggle:

- Sex, time, and money are cited as primary reasons for divorce.[27]
- 5 out of 10 men in the church are struggling with pornography.[28]
- 1 in 3 girls are sexually abused before age 18.[29]
- 1 in 7 boys are sexually abused before age 18.[30]

I've seen over and over again—in my own life and the lives of others—that untruths about identity and the shame that results cause us not only to segregate our sexuality from our spirituality but also to separate our very selves from God.

Intentionally integrating our sexuality with our spirituality does not necessarily provide us easy answers to hide within; it does raise questions and invite curiosity.

Integrating our sexuality with our spirituality is about holding the tension of both:

---

26 Newell, J. Philip. *The Book of Creation: an Introduction to Celtic Spirituality.* New York: Paulist Press, 1999. p. 88. Print.

27 Americans for Divorce Reform, Inc. Creighton University Center for Marriage and Family. Web. www.divorcereform.org

28 "2009 Porn Awareness Week." *PureHOPE.* Web. www.nationalcoalition.org/stat. asp

29 Childstats.gov – Home. Web. www.childstats.gov

30 Childstats.gov – Home. Web. www.childstats.gov

- The wildness and the wonder
- The potential to harm another or to connect with another at the very deepest life-affirming level
- The opportunity to enter into merely a physical act or an intimate encounter with our Creator

What if by hiding out in the safety of rules we have missed the truest identity of God?

What character might be formed in us by acknowledging and wrestling with our own deep longings and desires?

I am reminded of Lucy from *The Lion, the Witch, and the Wardrobe* as she learns of Aslan the Lion, who is king. She believes that he will keep her protected and safe from all danger. She hopes to find safety and that Aslan—in but a breath—will vanquish all her foes and silence the danger erupting around her. Yet, in response to Lucy's deep desire for safety and security, Mrs. Beaver describes a different reality: "Safe? Course he isn't safe ... But he's good. He's the King, I tell you."[31]

Aslan loved Lucy passionately and saw within her more than she could imagine; he saw her true identity. So, instead of simply taking away the danger, he walked with her in it. She began the journey with only having heard about this king, and as they partnered in these places, rich opportunities were revealed in otherwise dangerous situations. Lucy saw with her own eyes what Aslan knew to be true of her; she saw her true identity. She came to know Aslan.

Ultimately, it is the very wildness of our sexuality that has much to teach us about our Creator and about us as the pinnacle of creation. Like Lucy, we often want to be *rescued from* the dangers of sexuality and sex, when instead, it is our very desires, struggles, and temptations that serve as an avenue to walk more fully in knowing God. We interpret safety as the absence of struggle. God sees the struggle as an opportunity to call forth something that is deep

---

31   Lewis, C. S. *The Lion, the Witch, and the Wardrobe.* New York: HarperCollins, 1950. p. 80. Print

within us, from the very core of our being created—the image of God and what is beyond just safety, but "very good."

From within the holy tension of these real-life temptations and struggles, I have seen God revealed in awesome, intimate ways, ways that expand my heart and mind to things and experiences I'd never have imagined possible. In the words of Parker Palmer, "We can learn as much about our nature by running into our limits as by experiencing our potentials."[32]

Could we learn to view this vibrant, powerful part of our being as an avenue for experiencing God in a deeper way?

What if there is more to God's design for sex and sexuality than we ever thought possible?

Living from a Core of Abundance: Holy Sexuality

So, what exactly is Holy Sexuality?

Holy Sexuality is a journey of unending discovery, a quest to move forth with purpose into this wild and wonderful part of my being. It is to stand in the face of a world that has settled for a cheap imitation of the true nature of sexuality and to believe there is something greater to be experienced.

Holy Sexuality calls me to consider my sexuality an invitation from God; an invitation to be curious about the intentional God-given image within me and within others; to embrace my sexuality as a holy design. I am created in the image of God and specifically crafted as a woman.

Holy Sexuality involves embracing my physical body as a means of experiencing the abundant life of God.[33] It is manifested in how I stand as a woman in this world—spiritually, emotionally, and physically—amid the joy, pain, and struggles of life.

---

32 . Palmer, Parker J. *Let Your Life Speak*, San Francisco: Jossey-Bass, 2000. p. 41.

33 John 10:10.

Holy Sexuality is to value how men are designed and honor their unique spiritual, emotional, and physical composition. It is to recognize the image of God within the unique differences we carry. To love and value what God has created is an act of worship.

Holy Sexuality asks me to integrate—in a God-ordained way—what are oftentimes considered "opposing thoughts."

Cultural View of Sexuality	Holy Sexuality	Church's View of Sexuality
• Sexual drive can't be controlled • It's about pleasure	• Sexual energy as spiritual opportunity • Purpose and pleasure	• Sexual drive must be squelched • It's about procreation
• Deny the spirit	• Spirit+mind+body = wholeness	• "Deny the flesh"
• "Feels good = do it"	• "Feels good"+spiritual exchange = God's design	• "Feels good" = Sin
• Freedom-no limitations	• God's boundaries protect and empower	• All about limitations

- *Sexual energy as spiritual opportunity.* Our sexuality, whether as men or as women, provides a unique lens through which to view and encounter God. Its energy has incredible creative potential when we choose to acknowledge the physical power and also invites our spirit and mind to the equation. When we deny the existence of this powerful part of our design, we detach ourselves from an intricate part of our physical being. God can use this energy in powerful, creative ways as we submit it to God's authority and invite holy, healthy ways to guide us.

- *Purpose* and *pleasure.* God designed our sexuality with great purpose *and* for our pleasure. Yes, there can be tension for us in holding what are often perceived as two extremes. But God, as the ultimate author of sex, created it with great intention and with a desire that it be a place of fullness and abundance. "Everything is important. If you live your life intensely, you experience pleasure all the time … When you have sex, it's out of a sense of abundance, because the glass of wine is so full that it overflows naturally … you are responding to the call of life."[34]

- *Spirit + mind + body = wholeness.* God created us— spirit, mind, and body. When we engage fully with all aspects of our being, in an integrated way, we're deeply rooted in our true, God-designed identity. We live present to God's presence rather than seek to "find God." Being present to the wholeness with which we are created provides the opportunity to experience in greater measure the fullness of who God is within us and within others.

- *Feels good + spiritual exchange = God's design.* We experience the fullness of what God intended for sexual union when we embrace its pleasurable sensations *and* its very nature as a spiritual/emotional interchange. When we divorce either spirit, emotion, or body from the equation, we miss the opportunity to experience the beauty of the fullness and depth God has scripted into the sexual union.

- *God's boundaries protect and empower.* God established marriage as the healthy, holy context for sexual union with another.[35] This intimate weaving together initiates two individuals into a vulnerable state of sharing their distinct physical and emotional strength that, together, create a spiritual bond. When we ignore boundaries, we set ourselves up as definitive master of what is good. We limit truth to what we can imagine and define, leaving no room for the unimaginable and abundance of what God wants to unveil.

---

34   Coelho, Paulo and Margaret Jull. Costa. *Eleven Minutes.* New York: Harper Collins, 2004. p. 174. Print.

35   Please see chapter 6, where I expand on this.

Embracing my sexuality as holy has expanded my appreciation for both genders. It invites me to be curious about the physical and emotional differences between men and women without judgment and without feeling threatened by another's God-given design. If we see the etched image of God within one another, as men and women, everything we encounter and partake of provides potential for us to taste more fully of God's abundance and holiness as reflected in Genesis—"God saw all that He had made, and behold, it was very good ..." [36]—suddenly becomes an invitation for us to see one another in a creation-fulfilling way.

There is one place where our sexuality is meant to be a playground of exploration: in physical intimacy and sexual union with a spouse. We touch a sacred part of God's design when we lose ourselves in another sexually—fully giving and fully receiving from another physically. The power of a man and a woman joining their bodies unites them spiritually, emotionally, and physically, *and* holds the potential to overwhelm us with the presence of God between us and in one another.

The depths of this powerful sexual experience can never be reached in the context of one-night stands, which scatter our souls in bits and pieces and from place to place. Instead, sexual union is akin to the prophets entering the temple's Holy of Holies for the express purpose of encountering God. Ancient tradition required the prophets to place a rope around their chests so their body could be extracted should they lose consciousness or be struck dead by the overwhelming presence of God. Maybe that is why I once heard "orgasm" defined as "little death."

Physical pleasure is a divine invitation to experience the fullness of all our senses in a wild and wonderful way. "When you have sex, take with you to bed only love and your senses, all five of them. Only then will you experience communion with God." [37]

---

36 Genesis 1:31.
37 Coelho, Paulo. *Brida*. Pymble, NSW: HarperCollins, 2008. p. 124. Print.

When a husband and wife invite the holiness of the physical to engage their minds, God's divine presence rests between them. God designed us to be ever unfolding in mystery and discovery, returning again and again to this sacred place of union. God never intended sex to be boring or a rote act of procreation. Instead, it is to be an ongoing place of encounter not only with another but also *with the original Author.*

When a man and woman share their bodies in a sexual union, they share more than physical heat and passion. At a deeper level is an emotional and spiritual interchange that comes from the mystery we carry inside. When we acknowledge the presence of God in this very physical act, we are opening ourselves up to our truest identity and to the truest identity of another. There is a soul interchange.[38]

Old Roots: A Call to Reclaim Our True Identity

Often without knowing it, we allow lies to grow and mature in the soil of our hearts until we can no longer see God's true image, imprinted on us from the beginning. When sin or past pain takes root in our lives, it infests the landscape that is our natural, beautiful, God-given identity. God inhabits our sexuality and spirituality at their cores, but the quick growth of sin or pain blocks this beautiful, truthful view.

My husband and I live in an area that has been invaded with buckthorn. An insidious plant, buckthorn has crept in slowly and overtaken plants one by one. Not until we had lost almost all the indigenous plants in our yard did we realize how extensive the problem was.

We learned from an environmentalist that buckthorn was once valued as quick-growing foliage but has since become so invasive that it is choking out the true native plants and marring the inherent beauty of the region. The only way to reclaim the natural landscape

---

38   "Soul Ties"—while this term has been widely used in certain Christian communities, it is often confusing to many. I will address this topic further in Chapter 6.

is to pull this foreign plant out—roots and all—before it chokes out all other life.

When my husband and I first began tackling the buckthorn on our property, we pulled what we could see aboveground, ignoring the embedded roots. The problem is that when threatened, buckthorn responds by fortifying its root system. Each year, new outcroppings came from the very places we had cleared.

After a number of years of attacking our buckthorn issue—roots and all—we are beginning to see indigenous plants return to our property, and we haven't replanted a thing. The seeds of the original, inherent plants have remained embedded there and now have space to thrive and reclaim the space that was originally theirs. My husband and I now stand on guard against this foreign intrusion into our beautiful backyard landscape.

Although circumstances may have conspired against the truth of both our sexuality and God, the original seeds of God's true design rest within us and are waiting to spring forth.

Some Questions for Reflection

- What messages from either culture or church have formed and distorted your image of God and your sexuality?
- What does the concept and description of "Holy Sexuality" stir in you?
- Does the idea of integrating spirit, mind, and body more fully within your sexuality present an opportunity or invitation for you? What seems most challenging about integration?
- What do you long for God to help you reclaim around your sexuality?

CHAPTER 4

Differences Matter

Wholeness does not come in isolation. It comes
in relationship to the whole.
J. Philip Newell
Christ of the Celts

Question #2:

Are men and women really that different?

And if so, what real purpose do the differences serve?

Church and Cultural Points of View: Neither Satisfied Me

For years, I struggled between the seemingly opposite views of our culture and the church.

Our culture seemed to want me to focus on gender *similarities* and equality and to minimize any differences. "We're all equal and very much the same," was what society encouraged.

Church, on the other hand, seemed more intent on the *differences* between men and women, and used them to fortify men's roles as leaders and pastors and to minimize women's role in leadership and the church.

Neither provided fitting answers to the day-to-day struggles I was experiencing in my marriage and with other men in my life. I *wanted* to believe that the only real differences between men and women were our genitals and childbearing, but I couldn't deny these nagging, daily realities:

- Why was my husband's perspective so crazy-different from mine on just about everything?
- Why did culture seem to devalue my role and contribution as a stay-at-home mother, while the church elevated it?
- Why did church seem to relegate my leadership gifts to specific and safe "women" roles?

With no meaningful answers in sight, I determined that man/woman and the differences were one of life's painful, perplexing realities that simply needed to be endured. And I lived that way for many years.

My quest around this issue led me to a deeper dive into the truths of both scripture and science, which ultimately transformed my view of God, myself, and my sexuality.

From everything I've studied and learned, I've come to believe that:

- Man and woman—we both bear the image of God.
- God planned for both man and woman from the beginning and created us to provide rich community with one another.
- We must actively appreciate and engage with both genders to see and experience the fullness of God's image.
- God didn't mean for our differences to separate us; instead, they are intended to strengthen and stretch us.

- Recognizing and valuing our differences is to live in greater awareness of God's creative nature.

A Fresh Look at Scripture

Man/Woman—Created in God's Own image—Genesis 1

While studying Genesis and the story of creation with a rabbi, I discovered a twisted assumption that had shaped the foundation of how I viewed God.

> Let Us make man in Our image, according to Our likeness ...[39]

I had understood this verse to be about God recognizing the necessity for a *man*. What I discovered was how my perception of these pivotal words from scripture had shaped my view of God, gender, and myself.

I suddenly realized that my foundational view of creation went something like this: God made the man, soon realized there would be a need to make some reproductive means, and, therefore, created the woman later out of a rib. Woman was not a part of the original plan; she was an afterthought. She was needed, but was she wanted?

The original Hebrew text of Genesis 1:26 conveys something not at all reflected in my personal interpretation:

- God created using the image of God.
- The word "man" is more accurately translated "humankind."

In the original Hebrew text, this reference holds no gender distinction but rather gender abundance—humankind, including both man and woman! So, a more precise interpretation of this scripture is:

> Let Us make *humankind* in Our image, according to Our likeness ..."[40]

---

39 Genesis 1:26.
40 Genesis 1:26.

Humankind was created in the image of God. And from the very beginning, God intentionally wove them together in this original human form. Both are rooted and grounded in God's own identity. Each of us—as individuals and as genders—beautifully reflects aspects of who God is. Woman wasn't an afterthought.

George MacDonald so beautifully writes that we are created, "not out of nothing … but out of God's own endless glory."[41] God's glory, in its fullness, is displayed in man and in woman.

Where and How Gender Enters the Picture—Genesis 2

Both Genesis 1 and Genesis 2 tell the creation story. In Jewish tradition, Genesis 1 is a poetic cadence of the whole of creation, from the creation of light to humankind, and Genesis 2 is a more detailed account of how the man and woman were brought into being and of God's intimate interaction with them in the process. In a sense, the story is told twice, with two different levels of detail.

In Genesis 1, God sets forth a recurring pattern throughout the creation story:

> Then God said, "Let there be light"; and there was light. God saw that the light was good; and God separated the light from the darkness.

> Then God said, "Let there be an expanse in the midst of the waters, and let it separate the waters from the waters." God made the expanse, and separated the waters which were below the expanse from the waters which were above the expanse; and it was so.

> Then God said, "Let the waters below the heavens be gathered into one place, and let the dry land appear"; and it was so. God called the dry land

---

41   MacDonald, George. *Lilith*. Grand Rapids: Eerdmans, 1981 p. 147. Print.

earth, and the gathering of the waters He called seas; and God saw that it was good.

Then God said, "Let the earth sprout vegetation, plants yielding seed, and fruit trees on the earth bearing fruit after their kind with seed in them"; and it was so. The earth brought forth vegetation, plants yielding seed after their kind, and trees bearing fruit with seed in them, after their kind; and God saw that it was good.

Then God said, "Let there be lights in the expanse of the heavens to separate the day from the night, and let them be for signs and for seasons and for days and years; … God placed them in the expanse of the heavens to give light on the earth, and to govern the day and the night, and to separate the light from the darkness;

and God saw that it was good.

Then God said, "Let the waters teem with swarms of living creatures, and let birds fly above the earth in the open expanse of the heavens." And God saw that it was good.

God made the beasts of the earth after their kind, and the cattle after their kind, and everything that creeps on the ground after its kind;

and God saw that it was good.[42]

The pattern is this: God speaks something into existence and then separates out companion counterparts from within what has been created. There is an expansion that takes place: what has first been interwoven is now distinctly separated out. Dividing the light from the darkness, the heavens from the earth, the land from the sea, the

---

42   Genesis 1:3–25.

night from the day, birds from fish and animals that were created with companion counterparts. There is a harmony revealed by the presence of both, an expansion that causes us to remember their origin rests in being created to counter one another.

Can you see the pattern? Do you feel the building crescendo?

Skipping forward in the story, man's gender is first revealed in Genesis 2:23. It is when the woman who is his counterpart stands before him that he sees with fullness who he himself is and proclaims:

"This is now bone of my bones and flesh of my flesh, she shall be called woman because she was taken out of *man*."[43]

Just as we know light because we know darkness, so the man knows more fully that he is man by seeing the image of woman—his counterpart. Humankind is created in the image of God. Then God divided out the complementary aspects of this in-God's-image human.

This passage might make us wonder anew about the physical form this humankind took prior to the woman being extracted. I admit that at times I fight against the mystery and seek to make it tidy, uncomplicated, and quite buttoned up. What scripture does tell us is that the woman was taken out and that, as she was revealed, the man's eyes were able to see more.

It comforts me that for thousands of years, people have wrestled with the mysteries of God; I am not alone. What if the gift is the journey *within* the mystery? How do the questions continue to teach us?

Yet, there is more. Let's dig even deeper into what many of us might see as the familiar story of creation and discover what it says about man and woman.

---

43   Genesis 2:23, emphasis mine. This is the first time that the male gender appears in the original Hebrew.

The Man—"yāşar"

According to Genesis 2:7, God took ordinary dirt and, "formed man (humankind) ... and breathed into his nostrils the breath of life; and man (humankind) became a living being."

The Hebrew verb for "formed" is "yāşar," whose primary meaning is "to cut or frame."[44] It is a strong but simple, straightforward verb that is absent a lot of nuance. Yāşar is used in reference to the crafting of weapons, the forging of metal, and the act of sculpting. Just as a potter sculpts clay into a vessel, so God sculpted man in scripture's account of creation. I'm reminded of the familiar words of Isaiah 64:8: "We are the clay and You are our potter; and all of us are the work of Your hand."

This, God's foundational crafting session of humankind, Genesis 2:15 tells us takes place outside the garden. The formation of the original humankind form—though mysterious—is also profoundly clear. Man was formed in the image of God, holding within the sacred counterpoint of woman. While humankind held the essence of both, it was the woman who would be "fashioned out" later in an equally mysterious but distinct and intimate way. This was the man, but absent the woman as his physical counterpoint, the need for one another was yet to be revealed. Humankind held the identity of both man and woman.

In a very practical, hands-on way, God gets down in the dirt and sculpts from the earth—creating in the image of God. This creative step suggests that while God was creating humankind, there was also a very intentional crafting of the man, in a rugged and tender way: face-to-face, using the earth as a palate and God's image as the model.

Matthew Henry's commentary makes this reference to man's crafting: "He was not made of gold-dust, powder of pearl or diamond

---

44   Baker, Warren and Carpenter, Eugene. *The Complete Word Study Dictionary: Old Testament.* (3335). Chattanooga, TN: AMG, 2003. p. 465. Print.

dust, but common dust, dust of the ground."[45] There is a simplicity and a freedom in knowing that the origin of mankind rests in the palm of the Creator's hand.

Men and women were created in unique ways, with unique features and aspects to bear the image of God "as a whole." Science now recognizes the profound "complementary" differences that mark our brains, our muscular structures, and even the ways we respond to situations and the world.[46] While scientists are being surprised by these newfound distinctions, scripture and the creation story seem reinforced and further punctuated by them.

Are we curious about these differences? Can we embrace what is being revealed in both scripture and science as mysterious and sacred revelations of God's intimate design?

If we make space to value and respect both men and women—both intentionally made in the image of God—we also allow the mystery to expand our view *of God* and our relationship *with God*.

A Companion: Strong and Resourceful "Helper"

On the heels of working with humankind to name the animals, God proclaims in Genesis 2:18:

> "It is not suitable for man (humankind) to be alone,
> I will make a helper suitable for him."

We can only imagine what it was like for humankind to see God's creative animal display brought forward one by one. The experience was no doubt visually inspiring. But perhaps as the parade poured forth it also became disarming to see the animals in pairs—each with a counterpart and companion. Did a longing arise from deep within the human being? Does humankind have a counterpoint? What would that look like?

---

45 Henry, Matthew, and Leslie F. Church. *Commentary on the Whole Bible: Genesis to Revelation.* Grand Rapids: Zondervan. 1992. p. 6.

46 Did you know that a recent study found that men's and women's brains respond in totally opposite ways during orgasm?

Herein lies an innocent but intimate question at the heart of us all: "Do you see me?" From within humankind came a desire to not only be seen but to see more of what God would call forth through the awareness of needing one another—man and woman. Perhaps the deepest awakening and awareness was the longing for someone to partner with and the desire to be fully seen.

The stage is set for God to reveal an expansive plan for companionship—the woman.

"I will make him a *helper* suitable …"[47]

The full meaning of "helper" in this reference is complicated, and to say that something has been lost in the translation from the original Hebrew text is an understatement.[48]

"Helper" is actually a second-generation translation of the original Hebrew reference, "'ēzer kenegdo." A more accurate translation of this word is "help-meet," whose meaning is far more rich and significant for both woman and man.

Help, or 'ēzer,[49] means "one who gives aid."[50] The word "'ēzer" occurs twenty-one times in the Old Testament: two times in reference to the woman, three times in reference to kings and their armies, and sixteen times in reference to God, as when the psalmist writes:

> "I will lift up my eyes to the mountains; from where shall my help ['ēzer] come? My help ['ēzer] comes from the Lord, who made heaven and earth. He will not allow my foot to slip; He who keeps you will not slumber. Behold, He who keeps Israel will neither slumber nor sleep."[51]

---

47 Genesis 2:18.
48 OK, I am a woman, and I can admit that I am *extremely* complicated.
49 *Ezer* is pronounced "a zer" with a long a, like in savor.
50 Baker, Warren and Carpenter, Eugene. *The Complete Word Study Dictionary: Old Testament.* (5828). Chattanooga, TN: AMG, 2003. p. 822. Print.
51 Psalm 121:1–4 (NASB); brackets mine.

This word reflects both strength and a warrior quality; there is no connotation of weakness in this original Hebrew reference. This has far-reaching implications for women and is certainly a vast difference from my foundational assumption of the "helper" woman as being a weaker assistant!

Earth has always been a war zone.[52] God created the woman with a mission that reaches into every relationship, season, and walk of life. Her strength was not in question. It was needed for humanity to exist fully and with completeness. Man and woman were each given strength and were meant to share their strength, not to use it against one another.

"Meet" is derived from the original Hebrew word "*kenegdo*."[53] This term's component parts are incredibly rich in symbol and meaning:

- "Ke" means "like" or "as."
- "O" is a pronoun referring to "him" (the man).
- The middle letters are the Hebrew word "*neged*,"[54] which means "conspicuous, face-to-face, opposite to, corresponding to."[55]

In the beautiful words of Shannon Staiger, a therapist and friend who has done master's-level research on ʻēzer kenegdo and teaches within Jewish communities, "kenegdo" may be defined this way:

> This gives us a picture of the man and woman as sharing a common identity but not identical, they are similar but also separate and distinct, and so they are face to face where they can see each other. They can see their commonality and they can see their differences. More importantly, in their posture

---

52 Car James, Carolyn. *Lost Women of the Bible: Finding Strength and Significance Through Their Stories.* Grand Rapids: Zonervan. p. 36olyn James, *Lost Women of the Bible*, p. 36.

53 Kenegdo is pronounced "ken egg doe."

54 Neged is pronounced like naked, except with a g.

55 Baker, Warren and Carpenter, Eugene, *The Complete Word Study Dictionary: Old Testament.* (5048). Chattanooga, TN: AMG, 2003. p. 704.

of being face-to-face they are looking through the
very presence of God who is between them, giving
them understanding of who they are to each other
and how they bear the image of God.[56]

Men and women were designed to be a strong help to one another,
not be fighting over who is more powerful. We both bear an image
rooted in our Creator. We taste more fully of who God is when we
dare to see one another as vital to our own existence. Beyond just
marriage, by being in relationship together—man and woman—we
have the opportunity to reflect the image of God in a more expanded
way. When we bring the fullness of who we are—man or woman—
to the fullness of another and dare to see God between us, we taste
the truest essence of God.

The Woman—"bānāh"

God chooses to bring forth the woman in a different manner than
crafting the man. While the man was physically formed from the
ground, the woman holds the distinction of being the only part
of God's creation that was derived from what had already been
formed.

> So God caused the man (humankind) to go into a
> deep sleep and took a portion of his body[57] … God
> fashioned into a woman the rib which was taken
> from the man (humankind).[58]

Up to this point within the text, the essence of woman was intricately
interwoven within humankind. From having been formed within
another, she knew the Creator's hand that was now bringing her
forth. Woman was far more than a helper; she was a help-meet with
the man. In being drawn out from another, the creation of God was

---

56 Shannon Staiger is a counselor in the field of psychology and my friend. She has
    generously shared her research with me.
57 Genesis 2:21.
58 Genesis 2:22.

being expanded to reveal more. She bore God's image to partner and co-rule with man over all God had created. She was ezer.

The Hebrew verb for "fashioned" is "*bānāh*,"[59] which means "to build, build up, rebuild, construct."[60] Bānāh reflects intricacy and is used in the Old Testament to describe the construction of the Temple and the city of Jerusalem.

A number of years ago, while sitting in the framed structure of a house some friends were building, we looked through the complicated pages of their house plans. I began to see the differences of men and women in a much more practical way.

The structural frame is foundational to the stability of a house. Pouring the concrete foundation and framing with studs and joists are all done with a rugged precision that is essential. The framed structure serves an equally necessary counterpoint to all the intricate details that will follow.

Next come myriad details that depend on the strength and accuracy of the structure. Miles of wires conduct electricity, hundreds of sheetrock panels line the walls that are waiting to be covered in colors of paint. It is the frame partnered with all the details that jointly make a house. From the inception of the house plans, everything was necessary, each element built on the next. All the elements work together to create a place of beauty and protection. *All are vital.* The beauty comes when distinctions are no longer necessary and we celebrate the end result—a home.

Men and women are different. From the beginning, God formed and fashioned within each of us aspects of the image of God, which we carry in unique ways. From a man and woman's muscle structure to their varying brain patterns, science is recognizing and revealing striking gender differences.

What might these differences have to teach us about God?

---

59 Banah is pronounced "fan a" but with a b.
60 Baker, Warren and Carpenter, Eugene. *The Complete Word Study Dictionary: Old Testament.* (1129). Chattanooga, TN: AMG, 2003. p. 145..

Differences Are Real and Meaningful—Science Is Proving It

The lowest grade I ever received in school was in science. Mr. Fuller tried to impart to me an understanding of biology, but— unfortunately for both him and me—he didn't succeed. Thinking back on that class is still rather painful for me; it included many embarrassing moments and a well-worn path to the principal's office. But in my adult quest to better understand man/woman differences, science has become a new and fascinating friend. The new insights emerging there have much to teach us.

For years, science has studied the man's body and made related assumptions about the woman's body. Beyond the obvious differences in reproductive organs and genitalia, little research warranted recognition. In fact, in the Middle Ages it was considered inappropriate to use a woman's body for dissection and scientific exploration.

The study of women's health has exploded in the last century. And as a result, science is recognizing profound differences in physiology, emotions, and sexuality of men and women. Here are just a few examples:

Man	Woman
• Bigger brain/heart	• Smaller brain/heart
• Spotlight vision	• Floodlight vision
• Suppress pain	• Endure pain
• Shorter life span	• Longer life span
• Exposed genitals	• Hidden genitals
• Testosterone	• Estrogen
• Steady hormones	• Fluctuating hormones

While it would be great to explore all of these, we'll just stick to digging deeper into some of the core physiological man/woman differences.

Brain Differences

The brain is the powerhouse of our body. It's a three-pound mega-processor that explores and stores how we view the world and respond to it. The brain's two hemispheres (right and left) are connected and talk to one another, but in strikingly different ways for men and women.

Women's brains are more interconnected, and men's brains are more compartmentalized. The woman's brain has more nerve cells with which to connect its two hemispheres. As a result of this connection, women generally have the capacity to track and absorb from multiple information sources simultaneously, and their brains are better able to correlate a piece of information with the bigger picture.

Because men's brains are more compartmentalized, they are generally better able to focus on one topic at a time—like boxes that are opened, explored, and then categorized and stored away until needed again. As a result of their brain structure, men are less likely to simultaneously process information from multiple sources.

Mind you, neither brain is better than the other; both carry unique ways of processing information and the world.

As a result of my studies, I often say that women's brains are like a six-lane highway, while men's are like a one-lane dirt road; both are great ways to travel, but each gender will experience the journey in different ways.

On the other hand, men's brains and hearts are bigger than women's. Does that make them better? We live in a culture that would say bigger is better, from houses to breasts to brains. But while women's brains are smaller and more condensed, they are more efficient in how they process information and are continually active. Men's brains have more space within them and can actually experience "mental silence." According to an article written by Dr. Daniel Amen, author of the book *Sex on the Brain* and a world leader in applying brain-imaging science to clinical practice:

Neuropsychologist Ruben Gur of the University of Pennsylvania used brain scans to show that when a man's brain is in a resting state, at least 70 percent of his brain is shut down. On the other hand, when women were resting at least 90 percent of their brain was active, confirming that women are always thinking.[61]

I was five months pregnant and on a road trip north with my husband. He was driving sixty-five miles an hour, and our conversation waned to silence. The life within me stirred and I began to wonder:

- Is it a boy or a girl?
- Who will the baby look like?
- Where will we go on vacation as a family?
- Will we travel this road some day with him or her?
- What dangers will we face?
- Will we be good parents?
- How in the world will we navigate the future with this child?

To take a break from my own swirling thoughts, I asked my husband, "What are you thinking?"

"Nothing."

"You can't be thinking of nothing. You're driving sixty-five miles an hour. Are you thinking about the car, the road, the scenery, our future ... what?"

After a long pause, he responded with clear, familiar words: "No, I'm actually thinking of nothing."

Men actually do have the ability to think of absolutely nothing and still function. This is an unimaginable feat for a woman's brain and has also been a source of many frustrating conversations between my husband and me over the years.

---

61   Amen, Daniel. *"Sex on the Brain." Health Information, News and Tools – AOL Health.* 28 Oct. 2009. Web. http://www.aolhealth.com

Nothing? Absolutely nothing? Where can I get myself one of those boxes?

Eyes

As a result of how testosterone is distributed throughout the body, men have spotlight vision; they see what is right in front of them. And their eyes are designed to catch movement.

My husband heads to the pantry to fetch a jar of applesauce. He stands in front of the array of jars and cans and yells back, "Where is it? I don't see it anywhere on the shelf."

I respond that it is on the second shelf, next to the black beans, to which I hear, "I don't see it." I walk down, reach out, and touch the applesauce jar. He smiles and responds, "There it is." Because he now realizes that his eyes are trained to catch movement, of late, he jokingly does a jogging in place motion when searching the pantry shelves.

Women's eyes have more floodlight vision, which allows them to see a broader picture and greater expanse of things. Women must work harder to focus in on one thing.

Truth be told, we need both to be able to understand and grasp the importance of details and expanse. Both perspectives are important and valuable.

Pain

Men's brains actually suppress pain, while women's brains recognize pain quickly and have the ability to endure pain for longer periods of time.

Pain is registered by the brain in a region called the amygdala, but men and women process pain in totally opposite sides of the amygdala. For men, because pain registers on the amygdala's right side, they're more in touch with pain occurring *outside* the body and less able to notice and process pain occurring *inside* the body. Women's brains process pain on the amygdala's left side, which processes things happening *inside* the body and is also more connected to emotions and the details. As a result, women's brains are equipped to process a wider variety of pain events—including the ability to register and store emotional pain.

One obvious manifestation of this brain difference is that men have tended to die from massive heart attacks. The internal symptoms and warning signs leading up to this catastrophic event weren't as readily recognized or registered by men. It was only when the medical field began to study women's heart attacks—and women were able to name early symptoms—that medicine could help men identify warning signs at earlier stages of deterioration.

The fact that women have the ability to endure pain for longer periods of time is a noteworthy distinction, given the fact that women birth children. Men are usually the first to agree that if childbirth had been a man's responsibility, humankind would have died out long ago.

Not Better, Not Bad, Just Different

Now with this understanding of men and women's differences, the question and the quest becomes, how do we view, handle, and more importantly value such clear physiological differences?

While visiting Ireland a couple years back, I found myself quite uncomfortable on narrow, winding roads and thought, *Why do they drive on the wrong side of the road?*

Yet, their means of driving wasn't wrong, it was just different from what I'm accustomed to. There certainly were some funny moments of adjustment, but the experience helped me expand my awareness and hold differences in a new frame: differences are not bad; they are just different.

Men and women view and process the world in very different ways, and these different perspectives can lead to some of our greatest struggles and frustrations. For years I'd believed—at least subconsciously—that if men thought more like women, the world would be far more rightly ordered. It's noteworthy that when I broach the same subject with men, they seem to prefer the idea of women thinking more like them.

We tend to want to treat differences between men and women in very black-and-white, extreme terms. Our perspective tends to fall into one of two camps:

- At one extreme, there is *complementarianism*, which would use the differences of men/women to justify men's role as leaders with power and women as helpers subject to that power.
- At the other extreme, there is *egalitarianism*, which would minimize differences and propose "sameness" for the sake of equality of men/women.

I believe we're missing the whole point. Differences are an opportunity for us to see a richer perspective and a bigger view of God and how the image of God sees and interacts with the world. Differences reveal the potential for an interwoven, beautiful harmony with one another. Made in the image of God, these differences hold the fingerprints of God. Differences invite conversations that help us realize we truly *need* one another—man and woman—to see a fuller picture of life.

It is late night here on the North Shore as I write this. The moon is out and shining across a glistening lake. The stars are brighter than anything I ever see within city limits. In fact, the stars are so thick and bright that it looks like a disco ball is sparkling throughout the sky. The sun and moon come to mind. They beautifully coexist despite their distinct differences in purpose and place. They partner in lighting the sky, although in very different ways. The sun sends forth penetrating light that warms the earth, sustains life, and moves all of creation through cycles. The moon alternately provides soothing light, sharing the sky with the stars and pulling the surf and other life forces into sync with its lulling rhythm. What does this beautiful interplay have to teach us as men and women?

Do we dare to see the image of God in one another and in the differences?

Valuing Differences

How can we learn to value our differences and partner our strengths? By listening—really listening—to men's views and insights, I've been able to see a broader perspective of business, relationships, family, and scripture. The world was not meant to be viewed through the lens of just one gender. "True creativity is ... something that calls for a commingling of strengths between people, rather than the exercising of a one-sided power over another."[62]

Multiple studies reveal the impact and value of men and women working together in places like business and government. According to France's Ceram Business School, "Several gender studies have pointed out that women behave and manage in a different way than men. A larger portion of female managers balances the risk taking behavior of their male colleagues."[63]

In a May 2008 article for *Forbes* magazine, Matthew Kirdahy referenced recent insights yielded from gender science and its impact on corporate leadership and reported, "When the folks learned about the brain differences, the workplace comfort increased, and the power of that workplace increased. 'It's not about the self, the individual man or woman gaining more strength. It's about them *valuing the areas where they are strong*. Then it's about them *creating gender partnerships* between men and women so that they are getting the assets of both sexes.'"[64]

Do we really, actively value such differences? After centuries of holding logic in higher regard than the intricacies of intuition and emotion, are we willing to make space in our conversations,

---

62 Newell, J. Philip. *Echo of the Soul: the Sacredness of the Human Body*. Harrisburg, PA: Morehouse Pub., 2000 p. 87. Print.

63 Ferray, Michael. "Global Financial Crisis: Are Women the Antidote?" *Chamber of Commerce Nice-Coted'Azur publication,* Ceram Business School. January, 2010.

64 Kirdahy, Matthew. "Women Vs. Men: Who's Better at Business?" *Forbes Magazine*. May 2008. Web. www.forbes.com (emphasis mine).

homes, and workplaces to recognize the need and value of these working together?[65] I wonder about what God envisioned for our bringing together logic and intuition to care for the Kingdom and one another.

As I've studied and explored these things, I hate to say it but I've been embarrassed to realize some condescending attitudes I've held. I suddenly noticed myself saying things like, "Well he *is* a man. What do you expect?" Ouch. How many women have fallen into the trap of arrogance, devaluing the actions and attitudes of men in our work, our families, our friendships? To be a woman does not mean I have a superior view or insight into life; it means my views are an important contribution to the whole. If I think I am better than, or even don't need men, I'm devaluing God and the intention that we together bear this sacred image.

Men can play a part in devaluing women through jokes and comments that diminish the God-given image we bear. I am often forwarded e-mail renditions on the differences between men and women, and while I love a good joke, I'm saddened when humor focuses on the negative side of differences and devalues the potential we have to create greater life and fullness together.

In confronting some of my own foundational beliefs regarding men, I've come to realize the power differences have to divide and distract me from the greater good of working together. But, when I'm willing to hold the "holy tension" of our often-polarized perspectives, I see with new eyes more than I could on my own.

I do not need to be more like men; I need to be fully a woman, with all my complexities. I am needed in this world as a woman! Men do not need to be more like women; they need to understand and operate from what it is to be fully a man.

Ironically, as we each value our own gender as a part of creation, more space is created to value each other.

---

65 Logic is traditionally valued as a male trait. Intuition is traditionally devalued as a female trait.

It is work to actively engage with the men in my life, to see their viewpoints, to share my viewpoints with them, and especially to work through the differences in perspective in order to find a unified common ground.

Ronald Rolheiser writes that when Israel's prophets were called to their leadership role in the Old Testament times, they were invited into the ritual of physically eating the scrolls, which held the laws. The symbolism was that as they allowed their bodies to digest the word, it would become their own flesh; so much so that it would become a part of their appearance. "The task of taking God to others is not that of handing somebody a Bible ... We have to digest something and turn it, physically, into the flesh of our own bodies so it becomes part of what we look like. If we would do this with the word of God, others would not have to read the Bible to see what God is like, they would need only to look at our faces and our lives to see God."[66]

Imagine if we feasted on these truths, digesting them into our thinking, valuing the differences between men and women as something good that represented the image of God. What kind of comingled strength might be released as we work together and value one another as sexual and spiritual beings? The potential is for the world to actually see God in a rightly ordered way. In learning to navigate these differences and their accompanying tensions, we are called to a deeper harmony with God and with each other.

Let's Return to the Garden ... Edenism

Ultimately, God saw all that had been made and declared, "It was very good."[67] Men and women are different by design, and these differences are a beautiful, incredible display of God's own image and creativity. Our differences call us to value each other's perspectives and tap into the very best of each other. Our work environments, friendships, families, marriages, and churches will be richer and better, because we will see more than just our own view. Not only

---

66 Rolheiser, Ronald. *The Holy Longing.* New York: Doubleday, 1999. p.102. Print.
67 Genesis 1:31.

that, but I believe we will reveal God's glorious image to the world be how we value and partner with one another.

For many of us, it will require leaving behind our polarized, black-and-white perspectives and overly simplistic assumptions. Might we return to the Garden and live in the beautiful, holy tension demonstrated there? Let us live out creation's beautiful depiction of:

- Men and women are equal, both bearing God's image.
- Men's and women's unique contributions meant to partner with and complement one another.

I've come to talk about this rich way of living as "Edenism." It springs to life for me as I close my eyes and listen in a new way to the old familiar account within Genesis and recognize the truth it sparks within me. Edenism awakens within me an anticipation of what the differences hold. And my view of God, my sexuality, and myself are transformed as I let the questions open and expand my perspectives.

In my emerging definition of Edenism, I see a place where:

- Men and women would see our unique differences as valuable strengths that reveal the mystery and vastness of God.
- We would value men and women equally and celebrate who we are spiritually, emotionally, and physically. We would all be free to reflect the strengths of our differences without shame.
- We would be free to create partnerships that contribute our God-given strengths and let our differences tutor us in new perspectives and more holistic approaches to cultural, political, and religious issues.
- Women and men would be free to choose roles from PTA leader to corporate CEO, and whatever roles we choose would be enriched by the unique contributions that men and women can make.
- We would see and value and celebrate—as we stand face-to-face—what is in another that is not within

ourselves, that one day, "The glory of the Lord shall be revealed and all flesh shall see it *together*."[68]

Edenism is a call to return to the very core of our identity in God, a call back to the Garden. To return to the garden is to invite a deeper dimension of God's image to impact and expand my own view of God and to truly see myself and others through the eyes of my Creator.

68   Isaiah 40:4–5, emphasis mine.

Some Questions for Reflection

- What are some of the views and assumptions you have held about men? Women?
- How has scripture interpretation influenced your beliefs about men and women?
- In what ways does the information in this chapter stretch or confront any views and assumptions you've held about men and women?
- How might God be calling you to value differences in new ways—at home, at work, in relationships?

CHAPTER 5

Sexually Single

I can never know beforehand how God's image
should appear in others.
Dietrich Bonhoeffer
Life Together

Question #3:

What does healthy sexuality look like for singles?

Sexual Beings

If I had to pick one area of sexuality that is most overlooked, undervalued, and oversimplified, it would be sexuality for singles.

I haven't always known what to do with the topic of sexuality and singleness. In fact, the first classes I taught on sexuality at my church were "for marrieds only." But, after the very first night of class, a woman sheepishly approached me and confessed, "I lied ... I'm single—but I really need to hear this." Tears filled her eyes as she asked that I consider including singles and then she left the class. Her vulnerable and courageous words challenged me to look at the dangerous assumption to which I clung. *What in the world do I, a married person, have to say about sexuality and being single?* I wondered.

How does God view singleness?

I grew up in the days before color TV sets.[69] All the images transmitted through our home TV screen were black and white. I knew the *Wizard of Oz* and all of Dorothy's adventures by heart, but I saw none of the rich, vivid colors that I can now see when Dorothy opens her farmhouse door or when she encounters the horse of a different color. Back in the day, I couldn't see or imagine anything more than the black-and-white pictures on my nineteen-inch screen.

As I began engaging in conversations with singles and listening to their courageous vulnerability, they were clearly describing a richer reality than my black-and-white answers could accommodate. I longed for this singleness-and-sexuality topic to be simple, but each of their questions revealed greater complexity.

Here are some of the questions I continue to hear from singles:

- Why should I save sex for marriage?
- What if I don't ever get married?
- What do I do with my longings?
- Is sex ever good outside of marriage?
- What does healthy sexuality as a single look like?

Here my sexuality quest took yet another turn, and Dorothy's pivotal phrase kept coming back to me: "Toto, we're not in Kansas anymore." As I wrestled with the conclusive answers that the church had given to me, I saw a deep foundation of pure fear: if we acknowledge anything good about sex or sexuality outside of marriage, everyone will be doing it.

The attitude that sexuality is primarily for marriage is code for believing that sexuality is only about sex. Many of us—whether

---

69   If you are under fifty years of age, this might possibly be a stretch of the imagination. Trust me on this one.

intentionally or not—hold the belief that sexuality is an issue that first presents itself in the context of a serious relationship that is leading toward marriage. We believe that if we just hold our sexuality at bay until "the finish line"—the wedding—we will somehow have arrived and can finally live in the fullness of our sexuality. The assumption is that marriage holds a mysterious key that will suddenly answer all of our questions about this wild part of our physical being.

I believe that sexuality is meant to be a lifelong pursuit of wholeness and integration of spirit, mind, and body for both men and women, regardless of our role as single or married. But, I also believe sexuality is more than just about sex.

It has been vulnerable single friends who have taught me much about this overlooked, often taboo topic. Their insights and questions have prompted me to hold new questions and seek God's wisdom in new ways.

I guarantee you there are costs and inconveniences to retiring some of our traditional black-and-white views. Some questions will make us uncomfortable. But what if by asking them and being stretched, we will be invited to experience more than we could imagine?

Can we be sexually alive and holy while being single?

Addressing the Myths of Singleness and Sexuality

The quest for deeper truth around singleness and sexuality requires that we dig beneath the surface of some commonly held misperceptions:

- Myth #1: Something is wrong with you if you're [still] single.
- Myth #2: Our sex drive is uncontrollable.
- Myth #3: Our only sexual outlet is intercourse.
- Myth #4: Marriage offers special fulfillment as "God's best."

Myth #1: Something is wrong with you if you're [still] single.

After creating man and woman in the image of God, the Bible proclaims the handiwork as being "very good." While we know the two were invited into relationship with each other, there's nothing in scripture that implies that marriage was meant to be the ultimate place of identity. We are created first and foremost to be in relationship with our Creator, not to use another person or a cultural institution as the primary means of knowing God. Jesus proclaims the greatest commandment to be, "You shall love the Lord your God with all your heart, and with all your soul and with all your mind."[70]

Marriage or relationship never trump our core identity: God's image rests within each one of us. If we use marriage as the primary lens through which to experience God, we're not only dictating to God how our life will best serve the Kingdom, we're missing out on what singles' vantage point and life experience has to teach us all.

When we glance back through history at some of the incredible Kingdom contributions made by single people, we see lives marked by intimate journeys with God that have had powerful impact.

Paul—This lauded man of the Bible never married, but he clearly found great purpose and passion in traveling far and near to advance the early church. His singleness was not his identity, but rather an important means through which he served the Kingdom.[71] His words to this day impact and guide our lives.

Corrie ten Boom—Single all her life, Corrie lived as a true example of what forgiveness really means. While in a Nazi prison camp, she watched her sister die at the hands of evil. Years later, she stood face-to-face with the officer responsible for this evil, and her choice of the moment was to forgive and love the one who had been her enemy. Corrie traveled extensively and served as a spiritual mother to many in modeling this truth.

---

70   Matthew 22:37.
71   1 Corinthians 7:7.

Henri Nouwen—Henri longed to help people respond in the unity of love and chose to spend much of his life among the mentally challenged. "My hope is that the description of God's love in my life will give you the freedom and the courage to discover … God's love in yours."[72] Henri is a modern-day father of the faith to many through the words of the more than forty books he authored.

Joan of Arc—A young maiden of France in the 1400s, Joan of Arc's gentle heart was open to the power of God, and she led an army's fight for their country's independence. Her story of courage and leadership has served as an inspiration to men and women for centuries. First and foremost, she chose to engage with the life of God within her.

The man and woman God created were called to rule over the earth and bring forth life in all its abundant forms. The lives outlined here—all single people—have beautifully and passionately lived out that call in creative, life-giving ways. Perhaps their singleness even allowed them to be available to God's purposes in ways that marriage would have made challenging, if not impossible.

Many of us long for marriage to be part of our life experience, and if that is the case, that longing shouldn't be denied. While marriage holds the potential of experiencing a oneness with God through physical intimacy, it can only be experienced when men and women first truly embrace the fullness of God's image within them.

To know completeness and oneness with God requires a heart that is continually surrendered in the midst of all that is—whether that be singleness or marriage.

Myth #2: Our sex drive is uncontrollable.

My husband is a Weather Channel junkie. If there's a storm afoot, he's glued to the screen. I don't share his passion, but one day while meandering through the room, I heard news of a hurricane barreling toward the Gulf Coast and was stopped dead in my tracks. The news

72   Enjoy this website as it has wonderful resources www.henrinouwen.org

anchor was extolling the benefits of hurricanes. What? How in the world can something so dangerous hold anything beneficial?

Here's what I learned. Hurricane-force winds draw plankton up from the very depths of the sea. As they swirl in the air, this plankton grasps negative ions and drags them back to the depths of the sea. The benefit? We're left with cleaner air to breathe.[73] A hurricane's powerful force can and does cause destruction and loss of life, but at the core, the nature of the storm's force is to bring forth and regenerate life.

I'm certainly not a scientist, but as I've dug further into the biology of gender and the nature of our sexual drives, I've come away fascinated by the complexities and unique differences between men and women. I am challenged to confront the cultural norm that is often laid down as fact, instead of looking for what this strong human drive has to teach us.

A man experiences three powerful, overwhelming testosterone washes over the course of his lifetime. The first wash happens in the womb, forming man's fetus's genitalia and establishing the connection between the two hemispheres of his brain. Testosterone then surges forth again at birth to help the baby make the arduous journey through the birth canal. The third major wash of testosterone happens at puberty when:

- With every beat of his heart, a boy's body produces one thousand sperm.
- It's very common for boys to have five to seven erections a day.
- Nocturnal emissions become common—even normal—and then decrease as puberty progresses.

Absent any conversations or understanding to the contrary, these profound physical dynamics can leave us to "dumb down" the sexual drive to a seemingly wild, uncontrollable beast. Yet this force—as

---

73 Weather Channel information from 2005 during Hurricane Katrina.

an inherent part of God's design—is part of what God proclaimed "very good."

Is there more to the man's sex drive than just an animalistic force?

What if the very wildness of the sexual drive has something to teach men about who they are as sexual beings and who God is within them?

Women's experience with hormones is totally different. Born with all their sex gametes, girls begin life with over three million eggs, and only four hundred thousand remain at puberty.[74] From puberty through womanhood, women's hormone levels flux significantly within each month's cycle. And because of women's higher estrogen levels and the fact that their brain's two hemispheres are connected differently than men's, less of a woman's brain is devoted to sexual drive.

What if the mysterious and fluctuating nature of women's sex hormones has something to teach us, as women, about the potential life-giving power of our sex drive?

Is there more to the woman's sex drive than just bringing forth children?

Certainly, the complementary nature of men's and women's sex drives is interesting, and it says to me that God had intention in both. I do not believe the creation or variation of sexual drives was meant to be a thorn in our side or merely to be endured, but rather as a means of experiencing the "otherness" in *how* we are made.

I am reminded of the beautiful Cherokee legend of a young Native American boy who received the gift of a beautiful drum. When his best friend asked to play with it, the boy felt the drum was too precious to share and shouted, "No!" His friend ran away. The boy hated hurting his friend's feelings and sought his grandfather's advice.

---

74 Gamete—a mature male or female germ cell that is able to unite with another of the opposite sex in sexual reproduction to form a zygote.

The elder listened quietly and replied, "I often feel as though there are two wolves fighting inside me. One is mean and greedy and full of arrogance and pride, but the other is peaceful and generous. All the time they are struggling and you, my boy, have those same two wolves inside of you."

"Which one will win?" asked the boy.

The elder smiled and said, "The one you feed." [75]

What is it that we *feed on* when it comes to how we experience our sexual drive?

How we choose to view and handle our physical longings and desires will determine the life or destruction of this strong force that has been entrusted to us by God. I do not believe that God would design sexuality as something stronger than we can control.

In the book of Isaiah, God shows the nations how to reclaim part of their heritage. They had been "fed" a steady diet of war, yet God invited them to see, act, and respond in a new way. The Israelites began to, "hammer their swords into plowshares and their spears into pruning hooks."[76] God transformed the very instruments of destruction into tools that now became implements of provision. The very thing that had brought death now cultivated life.

A single woman describes it this way:

> From time to time I experience a growing longing to be held and touched by a man. As this longing builds—often within certain points of my monthly cycle—I know to make smart choices about where to spend my time and energy. Something as simple as a kiss or a passionate scene on TV or in a movie

---

75 Newberg, Andrew and Mark Waldman. *How God Changes Your Brain*: Breakthrough Findings from a Leading Neuroscientist. New York: Ballatine, 2010) p. 132. Print. The same story is told in many different cultural traditions with different animals and wise advisers. The most recent book I have come across is the one I have sited.

76 Isaiah 2:4.

can fuel these longings in an unhealthy way and create something that feels unwieldy within me. By acknowledging my desires, using care in dealing with them, and allowing God to meet me in them, my relationship with both Creator *and* my sexuality becomes richer.

Our sex drive, when viewed as more than an uncontrollable urge, holds the potential to bring forth life and generate the "very good" that God intended from within the Garden. Ultimately, it depends on what we choose to feed upon.

Myth #3: Our only sexual outlet is intercourse.

While our culture would have us believe that the only outlet for our sexual drive is sexual intercourse, sexual energy can be valued and channeled in other important ways as well.

First and foremost, I believe scripture has something critically important to lend to this discussion. If we return to the essence within the Garden, we see a man and woman engaging first and foremost with God as they navigate their sexual awakening and sexual desire. Man and woman engaged together and commenced the process of getting to know one another fully within God's loving gaze:

Spiritually—aware of their Creator

Emotionally—recognizing their former connectedness

Physically—being drawn toward one another

When man first awakens to his sexuality—by virtue of *seeing* the woman and *recognizing* a relational opportunity—a couple things are striking:

- It is *God* who introduces the woman and the man.

- The man's response is to *God*, not to the woman.

I find this noteworthy, because the man and the woman stood before God as the first two singles here on earth. But, they originated as humankind—knit together as one. God had designed humankind with an embedded potential for life; then, with a creative hand, separation brings them into two distinct beings and allows them to see what was hidden to them but known by God. Listen to Adam's words:

> "This is now bone of my bones, And flesh of my flesh; She shall be called Woman, Because she was taken out of Man."[77]

Adam speaks *about* the woman, not *to* her. God is the only other one present, and Adam's response to the sight of the woman spills forth in conversation with the One who he knew how to relate to—God. Man is first and foremost in relationship with God as he navigates this new person, his new relationship, and his new physical awakening. God—their creator and introducer—is at the center.

This humankind-turned-man has been in relationship with God, working in the Garden, naming animals. When the "otherness" of the woman is revealed and is physically standing face-to-face with the man, relationship potential is revealed. "Man's counterpart stirs his soul to a new level of self-awareness. As she stands before him … he also sees himself for the first time."[78] The man is suddenly experiencing a sexual awakening completely within the presence of God.

Adam sees woman's resemblance to him and is drawn to her. He speaks of her not as a soul mate or as a companion but of what he recognizes as similar, but different. In Adam's draw toward another, the thrill of another's sexuality also reveals to him his own sexuality

---

77   Genesis 2:23.
78   Kass, Leon R. *The Beginning of Wisdom: Reading Genesis.* New York: Free, 2003. p. 78. Print.

as a man. He "sees" with new eyes what God has already seen: the beauty of man and woman holding the image of God.

The image of God holds the essence of both man and woman. It also holds the very real physical draw that is in them and between them. At the origin of our sexual desire is a longing to return to the Creator.

How can we then handle this compelling physical draw—in partnership with God—in practical, everyday ways?

- I know a single man who has poured his sexual energies into creating music and developing soundtrack overlays. Many a time he has chosen to take the desire he has been feeling and pours it into chords and musical phrases, arranging music long after he has dropped his date off for the evening. He has found that when he has dared to acknowledge his desire, he has become more alive to his music.

- Another single woman who longed for a relationship began to mentor at-risk teens. Instead of allowing the feelings of isolation entrap her, she engaged her mind/body in focusing on others. She did not deny her feelings, but she acknowledged and held them close, allowing her to speak with raw vulnerability to teens in their own decision process as regarding sex.

- A single dad with two young kids and a strong sex drive used the gym as a daily outlet for his sexual drive. He lost weight, gained a deeper understanding of his body, and developed new language to engage with his children about their own sexuality.

- A single woman randomly going through a security check at the airport discovered her severe touch-deprivation when getting "wanded" and patted down by a security guard. An intense craving for physical touch rushed through her, and she found herself able to recognize, honor, and acknowledge this as a "good" desire. After that, she found that monthly massage appointments provided her with appropriate healthy touch from another human being.

- A single woman recognized her deep longing to have a child. As time passed, she acknowledged and grieved this lost opportunity. On a regular basis, she opened her arms and heart and poured out love to the small children of a weary young mother. Though pain could encourage her to protect her heart, she chose instead to give, and she felt a connection to these young children that only God could understand.

There is no formula to these stories, but in each case, each person chose to acknowledge the power of their sexual drive and to seek God for creative, productive ways to harness it with intention. All people can walk with an awareness of who they are and how they are uniquely made. Allowing our spirit, mind, and body to be a part of our sexuality is to honor an intricate part of how God designed our bodies.

There is an invitation within these deep longings and strong desires to return to the place of being truly vulnerable before our Creator with who we are. To separate or hide from God is to isolate intricate elements of our original design. Our sexual draw to another can lead us more deeply into conversations with One who created these desires. It is an active engagement, seeking to understand and embrace this "otherness" of humankind.

If sexual energy is respected, valued, and channeled in healthy ways, it is an invitation to discover more of who God is and how we are crafted with exquisite beauty.

What if the power of our *sexual energy* could help us tap into *creative energy* within us that is just waiting to be released?

Myth #4: Marriage offers special fulfillment as "God's best."

"Happily ever after" has long been both a storybook and societal view of marriage—reinforced over and over again in movies, books, and music. More recently, shows like *Sex in the City, Friends,* and

Grey's Anatomy have championed singleness—using casual sex as a central theme—as the ultimate fulfillment.

The institutional church has done its own pendulum swings in this area. Historically and in certain denominations today, singleness/celibacy has been deemed the higher form of holiness and connection to God. The western church has tended to elevate marriage as the means of knowing God more intimately. I fail to see either indicated in scripture.

God's creative process in Genesis reinforces that the man and the woman were crafted in one-on-one intimacy and that we are created to be in relationship with our Creator—not to use our relationship with another as the primary means of knowing God.

Ironically, my honest conversations with both singles and marrieds reinforce that we have more in common than not. Our struggles—regardless of our roles—are often quite similar.

What might we have to *learn from* and *lend to* one another in these places?

Similar Challenges

Challenges of Singleness	Challenges of Marriage
• Feeling segregated/excluded	• Feeling excluded/isolated
• Desire for physical intimacy	• Sex doesn't always=intimacy
• Marriage=value	• Singleness=freedom
• People's insensitivity and assumptions about singleness	• Weight of responsibility
• Labels	• Plateaus
• Sexual drive/history	• Sexual drives/histories

- **Segregated/Excluded vs. Exclusivity/Isolation—** Have you noticed that we often tend to cluster socially with people in our same single/married role and life stage? Couples can tend to socialize with couples, leaving singles feeling isolated and excluded. And married people can easily get swallowed up in expectations of them as married people—that their spouse is their true source and that it's inappropriate to talk outside their marriage about the challenges they're facing—at the expense of their identity as individuals. Intentionally seeing ourselves as individuals before God and our single/married statuses as merely roles frees us to listen to and learn from each other in new, enriching ways.
- **Desire for Intimacy—**Embedded within all of us are desires for spiritual, emotional, and physical intimacy. While it's easy to think that marriage solves and meets all these needs, it's simply not true. What do alone/ lonely places have to teach us all? And, how can we support each other in seeking God—our deepest place of intimate connection—in these places?
- **Marriage = Value vs. Singleness = Freedom—**Let's be honest: for all of us, on any given day, either singleness or marriage can look most definitely like "the greener pasture." What if we could let the pros and cons be just that, and celebrate with each other when we're experiencing the richness of our respective roles and support each other in our struggles?
- **Insensitivity and Assumptions vs. Weight of Responsibility—**How ironic that cultural assumptions about marriage as "the be-all, end-all" can leave singles *and* marrieds feeling less than! By overemphasizing marriage, attitudes and phrases like, "How in the world are you still single?" may sound like compliments, but they actually imply something is wrong with not having a mate. And many married people end up feeling a great burden of responsibility to be "good advertising"

for marriage and oneness in a culture riddled with divorce. Regardless, living the daily reality of marriage or singleness can feel unsatisfying at times.

- **Labels vs. Plateaus**—For singles, our culture tends to turn events/experiences such as divorce or the death of a spouse into identity. There's a profound difference between having been divorced and living life as a divorcee, or having lost a spouse and living life as a widow/widower. How can we help ourselves and others not to let painful life events become our identity? And while marriage holds touches and glimpses of rich intimacy, they certainly are not constant. Real, rich marriages are riddled with plateaus and dry spells where commitment must be the choice and the bigger story. Both singles and married people have the choice to live not just in the identity of battles/struggles of our journey but in the bigger story of who we are in Christ and the opportunity challenges create to powerfully transform our life.

- **Sexual Drive/History vs. Sexual Drives/Histories**— We both have struggles in this area. Singles must wrestle with how/where to channel our sexual drive; married people must navigate what typically are quite different sexual drives in each spouse. And whether married or single, many of us have sexual baggage that we carry with deep questions about if/how to live out the consequences—spiritual, emotional, physical—and how God might meet and heal us there.

Single and married, we have much to learn from one other. We need one another to truly understand how to live fully as sexual beings. Sexuality is about sex, but it includes so much more than just sex. I believe it is time to leave our married and single corners and dare to value what we have to offer one another in the area of sexuality. We all share a common ground: we are all singularly called to a relationship with God first and foremost, before any role we take on in this life.

Holy Sexuality for Singles

So, we're left to consider ways of acknowledging and honoring our sexual drive and shepherding it in healthy, holy ways. There is no magic formula with the wild energy of our sexuality. It has power for both good and for destruction. God never intended us to be robots of response. As the ultimate Designer there is a deep intimate desire to be a part of our being fully alive. God longs to be invited into and engaged in meeting our sexual needs and desires.[79] Ultimately, the guidelines and principles that you choose will craft how you carry your sexuality integrated within your life.

Paul, one of the most famous single men, speaks words of encouragement and challenge to engage actively our mind and spirit:

> "Summing it all up, friends, I'd say you'll do best by filling your minds and meditating on things true, noble, reputable, authentic, compelling, gracious— the best, not the worst; the beautiful, not the ugly; things to praise, not things to curse."[80]

The Amazing Ways God Can Meet Us in Our Longings

Over and over again, Jesus meets people in very personal ways in the accounts of the Gospels. Despite the variety of methods He employs, one thing is clear and common to all situations: personal relationship and encounter is Jesus' very nature. When we seek God in our places of need—leaving open the very means through which God would choose to meet us—amazing things can happen.

There is no greater power than the words of those who have personally experienced the Creator's stirring of their spirit, mind, and body. Here are some moving accounts others have shared with me about how God has met them in places of need:

---

79   See Appendix A for some guidelines of engaging Holy Sexuality as singles.
80   Philippians 4:8, *The Message.*

- My sexuality had been defiled through childhood abuse, and in my adult years, I'd used manipulation to control the men in my life. When I heard the concept of Holy Sexuality, I realized with great pain that I viewed my body as violated and worthless. It was while standing ready to enter the waters to be baptized that I asked God if there would be a way to meet me in the innermost parts of my body and heal me. While submerged, I experienced the sensation of water rushing deeply throughout the cavities of my body; when I emerged from what seemed like a very long time underwater, I stood up and felt the water gush forth out of my body. I felt clean in the innermost parts and knew I'd been touched and healed.

- I had moved into a new townhome and, as a single woman, was feeling very alone and overwhelmed one night by the daunting responsibilities of maintenance. I felt intimidated by the future and extremely vulnerable. Could I really do this? Could I handle all that would be required of me? Lying on my bed, I was scared, so I asked God to hold me. Believe it or not, I felt a gentle presence and warmth gently nestle in behind me—like someone was spooning with me. I fell asleep with the warmth surrounding me and holding me.

- My husband was sent to Iraq, and we had communication weekly while he was deployed. I wondered how I could actually be connected to this man, who was thousands of miles away and in a completely different world than me. Totally unexpectedly, we were unable to communicate for a period of time and I struggled, wondering if he was dead or alive. One night I lay literally paralyzed with longing for him physically, and I heard God calling me to remember. From a deep place of knowing, I began to revisit images of my husband in my mind and our spiritual, emotional, and physical connection. Miraculously, somehow God "brought me to him," despite the thousands of miles between us. I sensed a danger that was a part of his life and instead of lying there, I got up and began to intercede for him in very specific ways. When we connected a few days later, my husband shared that he had faced one of the most dangerous situations of his life, and I knew that God had engaged me with him in that place. God had allowed the miles between us to disappear.

- After seeking help to free myself from years of struggling with sexual addiction, I wondered if I would ever be able to look at a woman as more than just an object to consume. I walked out of a business meeting downtown and from the corner of my eye, caught sight of a scantily clad woman on a street corner, obviously looking to be picked up. It wasn't until I reached for my keys to unlock my car that I realized my heart was filled with an overwhelming sadness for the woman. The work of the years to reclaim my own sexuality had unlocked my view of woman. Instead of swirling lust in my mind, I was praying for her to be set free.

- I am eighty-three years old and have been widowed for twenty years. My body still longs for the connection with another, and at times, it feels overwhelming. Over the years, I have been awakened in the night by a gentle physical orgasm without any form of stimulation. In these moments, I'm reminded of the holiness of God's design and touched by the tender gift of pleasure for my body. I consider these sacred moments "a wee kiss from God."

- Standing in church one day and struggling to stay focused on a conversation with a friend, I realized my male eyes were continually drawn to teenagers, whose clothes were revealing more than I needed to see. I suddenly realized I had a choice to literally turn away. I asked if we could move our conversation to another area of the room. A realization struck me later of a strength rising within that guided me when I was most vulnerable.

- I'd lived for years as a single mom, praying that one day I might have stay-at-home time with my son. My only idea for how this could happen was being remarried to someone who—for at least a brief period of time—could pay the bills. I had a fairly serious relationship where this scenario looked possible, but I had to choose against the relationship because of spiritual and emotional red flags. I considered my dream lost. But within a year, I heard God call me to quit my job and trust that finances would be provided. Believe me, I wrestled with God over what seemed like a crazy, irresponsible act. But, as I cried out in this very "torn" place, I heard God say something I would never have imagined: "I long to be your husband and provider here." By trusting in this counterintuitive place, God did provide financially in ways I can't even explain. One of the deepest desires of my heart—to have time with my son—became a reality.

From an incredibly generous and creative nature, God always chooses how to meet us right where we are.

Isaiah speaks of a blessed reality when our struggles are brought to God and met with amazing power and intimate provision:

> Each will be like a refuge from the wind
> And a shelter from the storm,
> Like streams of water in a dry country,
> Like the shade of a huge rock in a parched land.
> Then the *eyes of those who see will not be blinded,*
> And the *ears of those who hear will listen.*
> The *mind of the hasty will discern the truth,*
> And *the tongue of the stammerers will hasten to speak
> clearly.*[81]

---

81   Isaiah 32:2–4, emphasis mine.

God can and does meet us in our sexuality. The Creator is not limited by what we can imagine but is, instead, ready and willing to partner with us in our longings.

What longings are you holding and how might they be a place of vulnerability with God?

"Sexually Single": Whether Married or Single

Sexually single? The concept that we all—whether married or not—stand "sexually single" before God might seem a confusing oxymoron. Yet, as I've looked afresh at the Garden and its beautiful creation story and how God crafted both man and woman, that is what I see beautifully revealed there.

God crafted both man and woman in a distinct place, through a unique method, and with one-on-one intention. There was not the input nor distractions of another. God formed man's frame in solitude outside the Garden. God fashioned the woman's frame by removing her from within the man while the man was in a comatose state of sleep.[82] Each was crafted in an intimate, one-on-one with God.

For both man and woman, their very first encounter with "another" was an encounter with God. Each one's eyes were opened to see the face of God, whose image they bore. Looking into the eyes of the Creator, they saw the fullness of their own reflection. The truest essence of their identity was found in God's own image, hovering over them with anticipation.

That God created each in a unique way and in separate one-on-one places speaks to a deep desire for intimate relationship with each of us. We weren't created in couples or even in company—other than God's. So, the first man and the first woman were indeed single in their formation and fashioning by God's hand. Neither was involved in the other's crafting.

---

82 Genesis 2:21. The same word was used to describe Jonah, sleeping through the tempestuous storm while on a boat being rocked about violently: he was out cold.

To be sexually single is to live with an awareness of who I am before God and with eyes to see others as bearers of God's image. Our desire for "otherness" and our longings have much to teach us. God, as the Author of our sexuality, holds the capacity to weave together our awareness and our struggles for good. There is a longing to be in relationship with us, as we learn to live within the body—a holy temple—given to us.

Within the sexual interchange between a man and a woman and all the power our coming together can create—spiritually, emotionally, and physically—we catch a glimpse of the intent the covenant of marriage can hold, with God at the center.

While I am a wife, mother, pastor, and business partner, these are roles I have, but they are not the core of my being. To each of these roles, I bring the complex and mysterious strength and vulnerability of my sexuality as a woman. There will come a day when I will stand "naked" of all of these roles and present wholly before God who I am as a woman. No one will stand with me; the roles will be stripped away to reveal the core of my being: a woman, made in the image of God.

Some Questions for Reflection

- What are your attitudes about singleness, and how do they impact your relationships—both single and married?
- What messages have you assimilated about your sexual drive as uncontrollable? How has this impacted your attitudes and behaviors?
- Reflect on the personal accounts of how singles experienced God meeting them in places of need and longing. In what ways do these expand your understanding of God?
- Whether you are married or single, in what ways do you embrace the concept of yourself as sexually single?

CHAPTER 6

Sexual Longings

The only way to make the right decision
is to find out which is the wrong decision,
to examine that other path without fear,
and only then decide.
Paulo Coelho
The Pilgrimage

Question #4

If everyone is doing it, why save sex for marriage?

What We're Really Asking, and What the Bible Is Really Saying

Buried within this one question—why save sex for marriage?—are really multiple questions:

- What is it we want to save?
- Where is "the line"?
- Is marriage the goal for sex?
- Is sex somehow better in marriage?

Often, we think that scripture is silent regarding sex, other than just saying, *"No!"* But, as we come with our very real questions in this quest around our sexuality, there are scriptural passages and beautiful images crying out to be heard in their richness and fullness. Unfortunately, many of these have been overlooked or watered down, often because of language barriers and cultural differences that have left "the good book" seeming little more than a G-rated resource.

It is important to realize that while the Bible is divinely inspired, it has experienced some translation trickle-down. Remember the game "telephone"? Someone took a simple statement and by whispering into the ear of another, passed the message on until the final participant said out loud what had traveled through the ears of others to reach him or her. Some messages made it through pretty well intact, while others barely resembled the original phrase, word, or statement.

In the fifth century, when the Bible's sixty-six books were compiled into one, scholars brought together Hebrew and Greek texts that had been translated into Latin. Centuries later, this Latin version was translated into English. Today, we have the text twice-removed from the original languages. While this is not bad, it has created some language and interpretation challenges.

Structurally, the Hebrew language is different than English. One simple yet profound example is that when we see "The Lord" in English, it is written and interpreted as a noun. Yet, in Hebrew this same reference functions as a verb. Therefore, a more correct translation of "The Lord" would be "I will be what I will be." Suddenly, an understanding of God as Lord is more than just a stationary noun; there is intentional movement, an active and fluid verb. Returning to the original Hebrew text can expand our understanding of scripture and of God, and it also helps us recover some important, overlooked aspects and truths lost through translation.[83]

What if scripture has more to say to us about sex than we've ever given it credit?

---

83   I am deeply thankful for Rabbi Alan, a dear friend and teacher. He continually expands and invites me to hold the tension of culture, language, and geography that creates a vibrating pulse to simple words, bringing forth life.

The Five Pillars of Sex

Scripture addresses the obvious physical nature of sex, while it also speaks of the profound emotional and spiritual aspects.

In the book of Genesis alone, I have identified five foundational reasons God created the sexual act between a man and a woman.[84]

- Creation of life
- Oneness
- Greater knowledge
- Pleasure
- Comfort

In no way do I believe this is an exhaustive list, but it provides a rich picture from which to address our core question: why save sex for marriage?

Pillar #1: Creation of Life

> God blessed them and said, "*Be fruitful and multiply* and fill the earth."[85]

"Fruitful," or "*pārāh*" in the original Hebrew, is a verb meaning "to be fruitful, to flourish. It indicates multiplication and successful production of offspring ... or human beings." "Multiply," or "*rābab*" in Hebrew, is a verb meaning "to be many ... expresses God's original mandate for humans to multiply on earth."[86]

God really does mean for us to engage in sex to create new life. This "be fruitful and multiply" statement is repeated seven times in Genesis and is always referencing the multiplication of human offspring. I personally find it humorous and significant that God repeatedly reminded humanity to make babies. Yet, the story of

---

84 While these are in Genesis, there are many more reasons in other areas of scripture. Enjoy the journey of reading with an eye open to discover more. I guarantee you will not be disappointed.

85 Genesis 1:28.

86 Warren Baker and Eugene Carpenter. *The Complete Word Study Dictionary of the Old Testament* (1692). Chattanooga: AMG, 2003. p.222.

creation is a continual progression of God bringing forth new life. Each part of creation unfolds with an embedded potential for life.

All of creation is a continual reminder of God accenting the value of new life and what it has to offer to the wholeness of all humankind. While watching an interview with Dr. Yvonne Fulbright, a sex educator and author of books on this topic, I was intrigued to learn that science is proving that the very act of sex in a monogamous, healthy relationship offers health benefits and increases longevity.[87]

Pillar #2: Oneness

> For this reason a man shall leave his father and mother, and be *joined* to his wife and they *shall become* one flesh.[88]

"Joined," or "*dāḇaq*" in the original Hebrew text, is defined as "a verb meaning to cling to, join with, stay with."[89]

While this verse, for many of us, captures the climactic juncture of a wedding ceremony, the true nature of joining reflects progressive, ongoing steps to becoming one flesh. The ceremony marks and confirms the actions that have preceded it—and the actions that will follow continually. There is a process through which a man and a woman first choose one another and then begin to leave all that has been in order to create a new union that will join them, "like the scales of a crocodile tightly fashioned together."[90] The word "dāḇaq" reflects that the two do not individually cease to exist but become stronger by joining together—just as a crocodile's skin grows to encase and surround the body as it matures. In the same way, the strength of a man and woman's bond can continue to grow with each additional physical union.

---

87 Resource for leading scientific research on sex: www.sexualitysource.com.
88 Genesis 2:24, emphasis mine.
89 Warren Baker and Eugene Carpenter. *The Complete Word Study Dictionary of the Old Testament* (1692). Chattanooga: AMG, 2003. p.222.
90 Warren Baker and Eugene Carpenter. *The Complete Word Study Dictionary of the Old Testament* (1692). .Chattanooga: AMG, 2003. p. 222.

Each time a couple comes together sexually, there can be an interweaving and a deepening of their relationship that builds on each previous sexual union. The roots of being bound together are meant to fortify and build upon one another. Making love to one for multiple years can hold a deeper "joinedness" that comes from having experienced this intimate and powerful interaction on a regular basis. Exploration and creativity are meant to grow and flourish—something that no one-night stand or casual encounter can offer.

A Scottish clinical neuropsychologist, Dr. David Weeks, attests that most people who appear a decade younger than their years are engaged in active, satisfying, monogamous sexual relationships.[91] Sex is healthy for us when it deepens our sense of oneness.

Pillar #3: Greater Knowledge

> Now the man had relations with his wife Eve …[92]

"Relations," or "*yāḏa*" in Hebrew, is a verb meaning "to know, to learn … to discern, to experience, to consider.[93] There are more than eight hundred ways "to know" reflected in scripture.

At a minimum, this verb indicates the richness of our sexuality and the multitude of ways in which one could possibly "know" another. While I have spent thirty years "knowing" one man, there are endless things about him still to explore. Casual encounters or one-night stands can't begin to delve beneath the surface of who another truly is.

In sexual union, when a man enters the sacredness of woman's body, with vulnerability he acknowledges the "otherness" she possesses and his longing for another. He enters the deepest recesses to receive—spiritually, emotionally, and physically—from one who also bears the image of God, one crafted by his own Creator.

---

91 Referencing a television interview Dr. David Weeks did while referencing his book, *Secrets of the Superyoung.*

92 Genesis 4:1.

93 Warren Baker and Eugene Carpenter. *The Complete Word Study Dictionary of the Old Testament* (3045). Chattanooga: AMG, 2003. p. 420.

When a woman opens herself to receive another into her, she makes space for the "otherness" of the man, who is distinctly different from her. She allows access to the deep cavities within herself that mark her spiritually, emotionally, and physically. Lines blur as she actively engages with and intentionally receives from another who bears the image of God.

The sexual union is meant to be an unfolding exploration and deeper discovery, an ongoing place of fuller knowledge of another.

Pillar #4: Pleasure

> Sarah laughed to herself, saying, "After I have become old, shall I have pleasure, my lord being old also?"[94]

"Pleasure," or "*ēden*" in the original Hebrew, is a feminine noun indicating "sensual delight, ecstasy."[95]

While Sarah's laughter was a response to the seemingly impossibility of conception at her age, her words also reveal an understanding of the sense of delight that sexual union offers. Sex truly is meant to be a place of pleasure and absolute joy throughout all of our years. There is an abundance of delight when we fully unfold ourselves to another and experiment with both innocence and abandon in exploring our bodies' response to one another. There is wonder in engaging so vulnerably with another through the years of struggles and triumphs, joys and sorrows that build a storehouse of memories.

God's generosity toward pleasure is abundantly clear when we remember the clitoris. This powerful muscle, strategically tucked within a woman's body, houses abundant nerve endings of pleasure. I often wonder what was held within Sarah's laughter: did she blush remembering the pleasure of previously being "joined" to her husband? Was she imagining and anticipating this physical time together?

94　Genesis 18:12.
95　Warren Baker and Eugene Carpenter, *The Complete Word Study Dictionary of the Old Testament* (5730), Chattanooga: AMG, 2003. p. 808.

Sex is meant to be a sensual adventure that holds rich and ongoing pleasure.

Pillar #5: Comfort

> Then Isaac brought her into his mother Sarah's tent, and he took Rebekah, and she became his wife, and he loved her; thus Isaac was comforted after his mother's death.[96].

"Comfort," or "*nā am*" in the original Hebrew, means "to comfort or console oneself."[97]

The sexual act offered comfort to Isaac, a grieving man. Grief is a powerful emotion that impacts the body and the mind, often causing a chain reaction leading into deep, dark emotions. During sex, the brain releases hormones and chemicals that stimulate the body's immune system. Sex can literally provide physical and emotional comfort. Over the years, my husband and I have found that the sexual union comforts us both—though rarely simultaneously and often in distinctly different ways.

> David comforted his wife Bathsheba, and went in to her and lay with her.[98]

I am reminded of the burning tears on my cheeks as I returned home, aching with grief after the death of my beloved father. I desperately needed the help of my husband to feel something besides the overwhelming tsunami of pain in losing friend, and mentor. Through the sexual union, my spirit and body were reminded that the grief that threatened to consume me would not prevail.

Sexual union has the power to comfort us emotionally and to remind us in a deeper way that we are truly interwoven spiritual, emotional,

---

96 Genesis 24:67
97 Warren Baker and Eugene Carpenter. *The Complete Word Study Dictionary of the Old Testament* (5162). Chattanooga: AMG, 2003. p. 723.
98 2 Samuel 12:24.

and physical beings. It is a vulnerable state to allow a mutually generated power to pass between two human beings.

Rightly ordered sexual union has the dynamic power to generate healing effects within the body.[99]

The Five Pillars: An Invitation and Opportunity

Together, these five pillars of sexual union reveal a deeper view of the spiritual, emotional, and physical potential of sexual intercourse. There is an inner landscape of support and strength that sexual union can provide between one man and one woman throughout the course of a lifetime.

When we value one element at the exclusion of others, we create something we serve rather than it serving us, and we have a foundation that lacks strength and support. Culture reinforces that sexuality is no more than sex without strings—one-night stands with momentary satisfaction as the only goal. Even many within marriage think of sex as being purely about pleasure, thereby missing out on the richness and fullness of all that God made available for us to experience. It is no wonder we have lost the essence of the sacredness of sexual union. We have traded the sensuousness of our sexuality for the physical trap of seduction.

A one-night stand or a casual encounter can never hold the seemingly polar tensions of comfort and pleasure, of oneness and knowing. Instead, these brief encounters scatter parts of who we are spiritually, emotionally, and physically, with no true footing or foundation. Like the remnants of a reused Band-Aid, the bonding ability of sex outside of marriage wanes and wastes away.

Upon what foundation have we built our sexuality?

---

99 Healing elements are rapidly being uncovered through the technological use of the MRI. The hormones and chemicals released during sex have an important interchange with our immune system. To read more about this, I recommend reading *Change Your Brain, Change Your Body*, by Dr. Daniel Amen.

During a family trip as a child, I awoke to find us crossing the longest bridge across water in America—the Lake Pontchartrain Causeway. With no land in sight, I felt sure we were driving straight into the water. I remember expressing my fear to my father, who explained that because the bridge was built on carefully placed pillars deep into the ocean floor, we didn't need to be afraid. He told me, "A bridge well made can hold a lot of weight."

Jesus talks about the wise man building his house on the rock so that *when the storms of life* pound against us, the house will stand. The foundation Jesus speaks of holds and sustains, because it is a foundation rooted deeply in someone. When we build upon the ever-shifting sands of cultural assumptions or pressures, our foundation will be washed out from under us again and again.[100] As the Author of our sexuality, God is inviting us to look at our foundations and examine upon what we have built our sexuality. The invitation is to return to the One who is the ultimate designer of sexuality and sex, and the rich abundance of all our truest origins have to teach us: the truest essence, reflected in the Garden of creation. God has a deep, rich invitation for us to experience.

Will we settle for only skimming the surface of something that holds such depth?

The Profound Impact Sex Has on Our Brain and Bonding

While sex is obviously a physical engagement, science reveals that significant emotional and psychological engagement takes place in the brain as well. I am certainly not a scientist by any stretch of the imagination, but I have been incredibly enlightened and challenged by the research and writing of several key leaders in various fields of science:

Dr. Daniel Amen
Dr. Helen Fischer
Dr. Joe S. McIhaney
Dr. Freda McKissic

---

100 Matthew 7:26–29.

William M. Struthers, Ph.D

Their work is very extensive and often technical, but my hope here is to invite you into some key insights that can help us recognize important bonding realities that happen in the brain.

The brain is not a stagnant organ, but rather, "from before birth until death, the brain is moldable and adaptable. It is not a rigid, immutable structure, but an organ that can grow and flex."[101] Like it or not, our brain and all its fascinating neurotransmitters are involved in the sexual act. These neurotransmitters have the power to imprint and mold our brain, enhancing its natural bonding ability or hindering our ability to bond with another.

In the act of sexual intercourse, "commitment chemicals"—a kind of neurotransmitter/hormone cocktail—are released in the brain and work to bond the two people involved. [102] Two primary neurochemicals that cause bonding are oxytocin and vasopressin.

Oxytocin. This hormone fosters deep and cascading levels of bonding, and the brain cannot distinguish between a one-night stand, a serious relationship, or a marriage partner. Oxytocin is present in both genders but in very distinct ways. In women, this chemical is present at consistently higher levels, and a simple, meaningful touch triggers the release of it. While men have lower levels of oxytocin, it is orgasm that triggers a 500 percent increase of this chemical in their bodies.

Oxytocin is a powerful bonding chemical that:

- Is released and floods the brain during sex and orgasm
- Produces feelings of trust
- Affects deeper bonding with each subsequent physical union

---

101 McIlhaney, Joe S. and Freda McKissic Bush. *Hooked: New Science on How Casual Sex is Affecting Our Children.* Chicago: Northfield Pub., 2008. p. 29. Print.

102 Amen, Daniel. *Sex on the Brain: 12 Lessons to Enhance Your Love Life.* New York: Harmony Books, 2007. p. 63. Print.

- Has an amnesiac effect, blocking pain or negative memories

The bonding effect of oxytocin has been linked to feelings of generosity in men, making them particularly vulnerable to being manipulated by the availability or withholding of sex within a relationship. Oxytocin is what deeply bonds a woman with her child and enables her to quickly forget the pain of childbirth. This bonding chemical also makes a woman particularly vulnerable to staying in an abusive relationship.

Oxytocin bonds us in ways that are ultimately healthy or unhealthy.

Vasopressin.[103] Often referred to as "the monogamy molecule," this bonding chemical is predominately present in men and drives their bonding process. While the details of how vasopressin surges through men's brains are still being studied, there are some key things we know about this powerful chemical. Vasopressin:

- It is structurally similar to oxytocin
- Is released during close, intimate physical contact
- Regulates sexual persistence, assertiveness, and dominance
- Affects a man's bonding ability with both a mate and any offspring

For men, vasopressin produces a partial bond each time they have sex, creating bonds with each of their sexual partners. Repeated casual sexual encounters can damage a man's ability to have long-term emotional attachment.

Oxytocin and vasopression partner in the act of bonding. Like a river flowing through our bodies, these hormones enhance our ability to feel acutely alive, but on their own, they are value neutral. Hormones are to be respected and honored as intimate parts of our lives and relationships, but the values they operate by—the definitions of

---

103 Less studied than oxytocin, there are many vital statistics that are creating an increased field of study currently in science.

right and wrong—are an important context we must place around them. Without governing values and principles, our hormones are completely "feeling" driven.

In addition to these two primary bonding chemicals, there is a powerful concoction of "pleasure chemicals" that intertwine in the brain during sexual activity. One of particular importance is dopamine. This "feel good" chemical affects a sense of pleasure when a man or woman does something exciting or rewarding. Released in its strongest dosage during sex, dopamine creates synapse pathways in the brain that recognize pleasure-inducing experiences. Repeating the behavior that releases this chemical, strengthens and deepens the neural pathways that have been actively stimulated by dopamine and increases one's desire to repeat the pleasurable experience.

What are we bonding to?

All of these pleasure chemicals and hormones are completely value neutral, meaning that while they operate with purpose and intention in the sexual act, they are also in need of moral guidance. When one has numerous sex partners, this "hormonal/chemical cocktail" causes his or her brain to eventually view casual sex as normal. Bonding is happening within the context of casual encounters, but the bonding is more likely to the rush of feelings than to a person. Over time, this minimizes and damages the ability of the brain to bond fully within a committed, married relationship. Popular culture reinforces that many struggle with this reality.

In all cases, these bonding agents create actual nerve cell pathways, and what we have bonded to comes, "to live in the emotional ... center of our brains." [104]

The desire to connect is not just an emotional feeling. Bonding is real and akin to the adhesive effect of glue, "a powerful connection that

---

104 Amen, Daniel. *Sex on the Brain: 12 Lessons to Enhance Your Love Life*. New York: Harmony Books, 2007. p. 68. Print.

cannot be undone without great emotional pain."[105] These dynamic brain influencers send signals to our whole body and create a longing to be attached to another. In a long-term, married relationship, this hormonal/chemical mixture helps a couple bond through the experience of sex over and over again.

"Sex may engage our bodies, but unlike such bodily functions as excretion, sneezing and burping, it also touches our souls."[106] In spiritual, emotional, and physical ways, an interwoven connection is established between two people, like two pots of concrete poured together that intermingle, unify, and bond in powerful ways.

What Sex Is and What Sex Can Be

If we choose to view sex as a purely physical experience, in its most basic form, sex is:

- A pleasure-filled engagement of two bodies
- A means of feeling connected to another
- A bonding experience between two people
- A means of expressing freedom
- A means of experiencing our unique physical identity
- An exciting adventure
- A passion-filled release

Yes, quite frankly, those things could just as easily happen within or outside of marriage.

But, if we choose sexual union in the context of God's full intention for us—committed, trusting relationships where continuous, deepening bonding occurs—sex can be:

- A pleasure-filled engagement of two bodies *honoring the other's physical design*
- A means of feeling connected to another *through spirit, mind, and body*

105 McIlhaney, Joe S. and Freda McKissic Bush. *Hooked: New Science on How Casual Sex is Affecting Our Children.* Chicago: Northfield Pub., 2008. p. 35. Print.
106 Yancey, Philip. "Holy Sex." *Christianity Today.com* / Magazines, News, Church Leadership & Bible Study. Web. October, 2003. www.christianitytoday.com

- A bonding experience between *three—man-God-woman*
- A means of expressing freedom and *discovering a sacred gateway to God's love*
- A means of experiencing our unique physical identity *in the fullness of God's design*
- An exciting adventure *in discovering the depths of another*
- A passion-filled release *into the endless, unfolding mystery of God*

Here are some beautiful stories that portray these truths, shared with me and shared here anonymously, but with their permission.

A pleasure-filled engagement of two bodies honoring the other's physical design …

After six years of marriage, she had yet to experience an orgasm during sex with her husband. She loved her husband and wanted to invite him into some new ways of exploring her body.

She began the practice of taking him to his orgasmic edge but gently inviting him to not cross over. She recognized places on her body that were more responsive, and she encouraged and guided him in how to stimulate her. She honored his body's speed to fulfillment but also discovered ways to honor her own body's slower response. Their curiosity grew, and they found themselves enjoying and honoring the rhythms of each other's body in new ways.

A means of feeling connected to another through spirit, mind, and body …

She was seven months pregnant when premature labor began and threatened their unborn child. The doctor put her on complete bed rest and prohibited sexual activity. He retreated from her physically but served her every need. She longed for his strong, physical touch but certainly didn't want to cause him frustration at the lack of follow-through.

One night while stirring in bed, their bodies connected in a spooning position. She felt the physical rising response of her semi-sleeping husband. From her place of longing, she invited him to return with her to previous times they had made love—through words. They remembered, they touched one another, they laughed, until they returned to sleep—sexually filled and longing for more in the future.

A bonding experience between three—man-God-woman ...

She was a virgin. She had spent three months preparing her body to receive his for the first time. He was a former sex addict but had spent years reclaiming and restoring his truest sexual identity in relationship with God. It was their wedding night.

He came to her with caution and care, staring deep into her eyes and honoring her as one created in the image of God. She received into her the fullness of one whom God had created. In their first physical union, they experienced a bond that expanded them spiritually and emotionally and became, for them, a truly sacred experience.

A means of expressing freedom and discovering a sacred gateway to God's love ...

She was in counseling to work through the memories of a sexual attack from her past. Physical connection with her husband had caused her to relive these wounds and her sense of helplessness at not having a "no" to her abusers.

Once again, her husband initiated, and she responded no. As she rolled over, a gentle nudge from within asked, *Would you trust me and say yes?* She closed her eyes, entered into the familiar rhythm of physical union, and invited God to lie between her and her husband. As she opened her eyes, she saw her reflection in the pupils of her husband's eyes and realized God's love in a deeper way than she had imagined. She suddenly saw her husband as made in the image of God, and the past had no hold on their union. God between them became both lover and healer.

A means of experiencing our unique physical identity in the fullness of God's design …

They were both frustrated by their sexual patterns but didn't know how to break them. Although they longed to experience something new, familiar routines seemed cemented in place. They decided to drive the coast of California for a week and explore something new together. With little more than a map, a rented car, and a simple carry-on, they flew out a week later to San Francisco.

The first day they drove down to Monterey and found a quaint little hotel by the sea. They decided to explore one another's bodies in a new way, through touch and no sexual union. Taking turns being blindfolded, this couple explored every inch of one another's body, asking questions and celebrating their bodies' differences.

The week held many things for them, beautifully reflected in this comment: "It took me fifteen years of marriage to see how incredibly awesome God made this woman; all 5'6" of her is beautiful."

An exciting adventure in discovering the depths of another …

She was overwhelmed with work, perimenopausal, and overweight. The last thing on her mind was sexual union. Her husband approached, and she said—more than half-jokingly—that if he could find any part of her that could be aroused, it was all his.

The challenge was laid down, and she lay back and allowed him to explore her physically, with little to no reserves from which to respond. In the midst of just being, her body began to awaken to something beyond her feelings, and she felt caught up and swept away. In a way she'd never experienced before, she felt disoriented and outside herself. Her husband responded, "I see you … I am right here … I don't need a thing … just let me hold you."

Her husband later told her that in that moment, he experienced a depth in her that was beyond his understanding: the intimate power of just holding another.

A passion-filled release into the endless unfolding mystery of God ...

He was successful in his career, someone others sought for business guidance. His work environment was changing, and he suddenly found himself in a situation with his integrity being questioned from every side. Daily, he returned from work frustrated and angry. The kids, his wife, and his God all felt distant.

They lay in their bedroom, exhausted and frustrated by the chaos of life. Sex was, for him, a tempting escape. But instead, he invited his wife into the storms that were raging and asked if together they could physically and emotionally let them go.

In the aftermath, he found these words: "In pouring out my strength, your strength lifts me to a place that I cannot experience alone. And I feel Someone holding us."

A choice to pursue what sex *can be* is a choice to honor the healthy, holy boundaries God provided so our spiritual, emotional, and physical connection—to both another *and* to the Creator—can deepen and flourish and be enriched over time.

Myths and Common Roadblocks

Unfortunately, there are commonly held misperceptions that keep us from recognizing and entering into the fullness of God's design and intention for us. Before we can truly experience the fullness sexual union offers, we'll need to address three common myths.

- Myth #1: Premarital sex doesn't hurt anybody.
- Myth #2: Sex is the unforgivable sin.
- Myth #3: Once I am married, sex will be easy and great.

Myth #1: Premarital sex doesn't hurt anybody.

Casual sex is, by nature, more about taking or capturing something for ourselves without allowing another to share in the deepest part of who we are. Sex without true commitment does not allow for deep trust and the freedom to vulnerably abandon ourself to another.

"If we are serious about loving someone, we have to surrender all of the desires within us to manipulate the relationship."[107] As a result of the bonding neurochemicals released in our brain, casual sexual intimacy teaches the brain to be on guard and in protection mode for the eventual ripping apart from another. We cannot unfold ourselves fully when we live with the fear of losing and letting go of the other.

To engage in sex purely as a physical interaction is to miss out on the fullness of being known, to remain invisible in a world where we long to be seen. Sex as mere physical release can literally be a form of hiding from being known by another.

I recently saw a porn star interviewed on a popular TV talk show. She spoke of the freedom her industry has given women and men to explore their true sexual fantasies and the fact that it has enhanced the lives of many. But when the question turned to how her porn career had impacted her life in the (big picture) long term, this same woman teared up, speaking of a loneliness she always carries and the painful reality that she will someday have to explain her choices to her children. "No one will ever know who I really am ... I will always just be a porn star."

God is not against sex, not against pleasure; in fact, God is all for it and wants to be a part of it, not held at arm's length. God created us with deep pleasure capacities within our physical being. Because of the power sex has to bind us to another, the consequence of casual sex outside the covenant of marriage is often shame. The enemy likes nothing better than to use shame as a means of trapping us and destroying our relationships. "Sex has enough combustive force to incinerate conscience, vows, family commitments, religious devotion, and anything else in its path."[108]

---

107 Bell, Rob. *Sex God: Exploring the Endless Connections Between Sexuality and Spirituality.* Grand Rapids: Zondervan, 2007. p. 98. Print.
108 Yancey, Philip. "Holy Sex." *Christianity Today.com* / Magazines, News, Church Leadership & Bible Study. Web. October, 2003. www.christianitytoday.com

True freedom comes from knowing that the boundaries God offers are not there to hinder our progress but to provide and protect a storehouse of possibility when we stand with the One who created and fully understands the abundance and riches these boundaries hold.

Myth #2: Sex is the unforgivable sin.

Of all the lies about sex, this one saddens me the most.

I was raised in the church and have seen firsthand how sexual sin typically outranks all others and is deemed virtually unforgivable. Attempts to squelch sexual activity outside of marriage have fueled a culture of shame and fear, while suppressing the true relevance and hope that scripture offers. It is in Jesus' own actions that I see just the opposite: honest, straightforward, compassionate responses that indicate acknowledgment of and respect for this wild and dangerous part of our physical design.

In the book of John, there is a group of people so incensed by the seeming disruption and discord Jesus' teaching is causing that they opportunistically pounce on a woman caught in the act of adultery. Most commentaries believe the group actually set up this woman, given the time of day and the fact that they want to punish her alone and not the man as well. The Law of Moses instructs that both the man and the woman caught in adultery were to be stoned to death.

Imagine with me this woman's shame and confusion at being yanked from a bed of passion—barely clothed, I assume—and then dragged to the temple and tossed into the center courts before a male teacher. Questions arise for me:

- Did anyone have compassion and offer her a cloak?
- Did the crowd grow quiet, or did they mock her?
- Could she breathe through her tears?
- Why did her sexual partner abandon her to face the consequences alone?
- Did anyone who knew her stick by her side?

Those who threw her at Jesus' feet wanted her stoned immediately. They sought vengeance. We don't know if this woman was single or married, but in the early morning moment, her fate played out at center court in the house of worship. She seemed destined to experience both the height of passion and the depth of despair in the course of but minutes.

But Jesus' actions are a powerful counterpoint to those of the accusing band. Jesus stooped down and began to draw in the sand. There are many scholarly speculations about what and why He wrote, but I see a man who is both respectful of and feeling vulnerable with a naked woman in His midst. Of anyone on earth, Jesus must have been aware of the power and beauty a woman's body holds and how quickly that can get misused.

Might diverting His gaze be Jesus' physical response from a heart that chose to honor this woman? My simple theology is that He is modeling for us all what it means to have compassion and to look away when tempted.

Here is the part that most of us fail to recognize in this account: Jesus leveled any assumptions about a hierarchy of sin in one pointed statement.

> He straightened up, and said to *them*, "He who is without sin among you, *let him be the first* to throw a stone at her."[109]

Scripture says they, "persisted in asking Him," but Jesus knew the hearts of all involved. Gossip, hatred, lying, gluttony, pride, disdain, and vengeance were suddenly placed on the same scale. Jesus' own words and actions proclaim that sin is sin, not one outranks another, and grace is available to all.

The only one who could, in truth, throw a stone was the One who had stooped down and returned to drawing in the dirt.

---

109 John 8:1–11. To read the whole story and allowing the weight of the stones we carry to be released is a humbling engagement with God. (emphases mine)

Who are we to use a scale to weigh the sins of one another?

How interesting that to this day, we reference her as "the adulterous woman," despite the fact that when Jesus addresses her, He calls forth her true identity as woman—"one who bears life." He doesn't ignore her actions but asks her to name her accusers. As she looks around to find no one there, Jesus proclaims:

> "I do not condemn you, either. Go. From now on sin no more."[110]

What if the church was a place one could be so vulnerable?

What might grace look like in our families, communities, and churches today?

Myth #3: Once I am married, sex will be easy and great.

Religion often portrays weddings as a magical moment, when a switch gets flipped that makes the wedding night and sexual union infinitely glorious. Many maintain sexual purity before marriage, hoping on some level that "good behavior" will ensure endless, mind-blowing sex within marriage. [111]

Yet, little is done to equip men or women in the "how" of engaging physically with one another other than, "Oh, you will figure it out." Men and women often end up in their wedding bed with very different perspectives and expectations.

Here's a synopsis of expectations I often hear from women:

> The wedding night is something that I think about. Will I wear the right thing? Will he find me attractive? I want the sex to be magical, something we will remember forever.

Here's what I often hear from men:

---

110 John 8:11.
111 Sexual purity is often labeled as the absence of having intercourse before the wedding night. Does a black-and-white "line" trump engagement of the heart?

> The wedding night is something I can hardly wait for. All I want to do is rip off her clothes and dive into her body. We are going to do it over and over, and it is going to be awesome.

Truth be told, the wedding night often becomes a time when imagination and reality have a head-on collision. While both perspectives hold value, neither holds the full picture. Within these unrealistic expectations lie some foundational assumptions:

- Assumption—sex is simple
- Entitlement—"me" versus mutuality
- Soul Ties—sexual remnants of others

Assumption—sex is simple

Our present-day media portrays sex with such glamour and ease that we're left to believe that two bodies come together—bing, bang, boom!—and magic simply happens.

Very few people are taught about the fundamentals of sex:

- *Sex takes planning.* While spontaneous sex is a wonderful part of a relationship, there are not so simple things like birth control and time tables that often need to be considered. And while sometimes sex is more like fast food—quick and with little planning—other times it can be more like a gourmet meal—with creative ambiance and intentional stages.
- *Sex is messy.* When a man and woman come together, they bring their own unique body chemistry. People have different levels of comfort with body fluids, and sweat and semen alone create new and unique scents to experience. A hand towel, a breath mint, or a simple candle can add to the enjoyment.
- *Sex is more than just the time it takes.* The physical dimension of sex is but one aspect of joining together. Often, sex for men is about everything in the last four minutes (ready to go at a moment's notice), while sex for

women is about everything that has happened in the last twenty-four hours ("Do I feel emotionally connected right now?").

When we value sexual union and all that it awakens in two people, we engage in a spiritual nakedness that unfolds our body and innermost being to another. "Human beings are, after all, the only creatures which can be naked, the only creatures in which this bizarre unveiling can take place."[112] To respect and value the most vulnerable hidden parts of who we are is to open our eyes to fully see into one another.

Entitlement—"me" versus mutuality

They had been married six weeks and were sitting in my office with little to indicate they were newlyweds. He clearly loved his wife but was frustrated because sex had happened only a handful of times. "I can't believe that I waited for this ... I feel gypped." She was deeply in love with her husband but wanted nothing to do with sex. "It's just too painful. I thought it would be different."

No one had instructed them in how to prepare their own bodies and minds for sexual union. They had spent fourteen months planning the wedding day, down to minute details, and a mere three sessions with their pastor talking about their marriage—only briefing touching on sex.

Within many Jewish communities, it is common for a newlywed couple to spend the first year of their marriage meeting weekly with an older married couple. This first year is viewed as on-the-job training, and there's a recognized need to be in community in order to *create something* rather than just *experience something*.

In a number of ancient cultures, older women had the responsibility of instructing the younger men in the art of lovemaking. While I am not suggesting that we literally resume this ancient tradition, I am concerned about how far removed we are from instructing and

---

112 Mason, Mike. *The Mystery of Marriage.* Sisters: Multnomah, 1985 p. 140. Print.

equipping both men and women in sex as both an art and sacred union.

In the beautiful words of Thomas Merton, "Sex can become routine in marriage, especially if all the accouterments remain plain and familiar; but if sex is seen as an art rather than mere self-expression or duty, then the whole of one's life can prepare for it and at the same time be carried on in the afterglow of sex."[113]

Some helpful insights:

- Women: prepare your body. First-time sex is always painful for women.[114] Our brain holds onto the memory of pain, and like a hand pulling away from heat, it tells the affected area to pull away from what is causing pain. Vaginismus is a common side effect of experiencing sexual trauma. [115] Many women suffer from vaginal dryness[116] and yeast infections[117] that make sexual intercourse challenging, but not impossible. Having intercourse multiple times can actually cause the vaginal cavity to become sore and ache.
- Men: slow down. Sex isn't like in the movies, where a woman is ready to receive a man at a moment's notice. Women are often shocked by the size of a man's penis and immediately fear something that large fitting inside them. You are well acquainted with your own genitals; take time to gradually introduce her to this part of your anatomy, and get to know hers.

---

113 Merton, Thomas. *The Soul of Sex.* (New York: Harper Collins, 1998) p. 216. Print.

114 The hymen is a thin layer of skin that covers the vaginal cavity. A simple process of stretching this skin intentionally with fingers and a good lubricant helps with ease of penetration.

115 Vaginal spasms recurrent during intercourse that contract the size of the vagina, and create pain. Please check with your doctor if you experience these symptoms; there are effective treatments.

116 An effective lubricant can ease dryness and enhance pleasure.

117 If you experience repeated yeast infections from intercourse, please see your doctor. Simple things like changing your diet have been known to help.

- Sexual drives vary. Notice how your sex drives differ, but don't assume one is "good" and the other "bad." Instead, learn to talk about the differences and mutually share the responsibility of staying engaged and caring for one another physically.

"The marriage bed must be a place of mutuality—the husband seeking to satisfy his wife, the wife seeking to satisfy her husband. Marriage is not a place to 'stand up for your rights.' Marriage is a decision to serve the other, whether in bed or out."[118]

Soul ties—sexual remnants of others

One of the profound impacts of sex is that it unites us with another in physical and emotional ways that subtly and slowly impact us spiritually as well. "It may be tempting at times to imagine sex as purely physical … How pleasant it would be, we may think, to have sex without strings attached, without all the painful emotions … but the soul has its own life and its own will. It won't submit to our manipulations."[119]

Soul ties. My sexual abuse and promiscuity left remnants of others that were lingering around my marriage bed. I had knowingly and unknowingly fragmented my soul: some parts of me had been taken and other parts carelessly left with others. I began to notice the impact this was having on my marriage bed.

- *It limited my ability to receive.* The affection given to me never seemed enough. Like a cup with holes punched into the sides, whatever was poured in continued to leak out.
- *It hindered my capacity to give.* The division of my soul affected how much I was capable of giving. When holding but a half a piece of bread, one strategically shares smaller portions.

---

118 1 Corinthians 7:3–4, *The Message.*
119 Merton, Thomas. *The Soul of Sex.* New York: Harper Collins, 1998. p. 4. Print.

When I learned about soul ties and their lingering impact on the present, I realized I held the power to break free of what was weighing me down and tying me to another. With a repentant heart, I severed the soul ties, and with a grateful heart, I gradually began to experience something different. I was more wholly present to my husband.[120]

Marriage isn't a place of refuge to hide from our sexuality, ignore it, or assume it will maintain itself. Marriage is not a substitute for our relationship with God. "You can't be connected with God until you're at peace with who you are. If you're still upset that God gave you this body or this life or this family or these circumstances, you will never be able to connect with God in a healthy, thriving, sustainable sort of way. You'll be at odds with your master."[121]

"Marriage is to be held in honor among all, and the marriage bed is to be undefiled."[122]

A Choice to Make

Sexual union is a powerful force that engages our mind and emotions to open and share fully with another, to be vulnerable. We will never taste the potential depths of sex through sampling and experimenting with multiple partners. The very nature of sexual engagement is an ever-deeper bonding that builds within a relationship over time. To be further unveiled and released into one another—spiritually, emotionally, and physically—is a journey of discovery and is part of how the bond within a marriage is sealed.

I once heard Dallas Willard say, "We are spiritual beings having an earthly experience." Our spiritual roots can be traced to the Garden, and yet our feet stand here, upon the soil of a culture that

---

120 There is no perfect spiritual formula for this. It is calling back that which is rightfully yours and releasing that which is another's. I have enclosed a prayer at the end of the book if you feel called to walk down this path. See appendix B.
121 Bell, Rob. *Sex God: Exploring the Endless Connections Between Sexuality and Spirituality.* (Grand Rapids: Zondervan, 2007) p. 46. Print.
122 Hebrews 13:4.

would try to reduce our truest identity to something transient and transactional.

God's design for sexual union, as reflected in scripture, is that it be a covenantal place that will continue to bond us, shape us, reveal to us, pleasure us, comfort us, and join us to the one whose image we bear—God. Thus, God placed sexual union within the covenant of marriage: one man to one woman so, "the two shall become one."[123] This sacred boundary is not about keeping us from enjoyment and pleasure but about wanting to teach us about the truest, deepest forms of pleasure and oneness.

My husband and I were recently at a wedding where straight-line winds tore up trees and collapsed the outdoor tent. We left the reception to head home, with the storm ahead and clear blue skies behind. In the midst of this drama, we saw two clear rainbows, side by side, and it took our breath away. Once again, we were reminded that even amid devastation, God's covenantal promise endures, offering hope.

"Healthy marriages all have this sense of mutual abandon to each other."[124] A covenant celebrates the value each brings to the marriage and to the marriage bed out of the strength that each person is and offers there. It endures and prevails through the storms of life. The sexual union is more than just flesh entwined; it is a union of two spiritual beings, coming together to share this passionate, sacred, earthly experience with God as the Creator of sex.

Might our deepest desires lead us, in partnership with God, to discover something richer and fuller than we ever imagined?

---

123 Matthew 19:6.
124 Bell, Rob. *Sex God: Exploring the Endless Connections Between Sexuality and Spirituality.* Grand Rapids: Zondervan, 2007. p. 118. Print.

Some Questions for Reflection

- Based on the scriptural and scientific insights shared in this chapter, are you prompted to think differently about sexual union?
- What does Jesus' response to the woman caught in adultery say to you about sexual sin? Does this have implications for your own history/experience or attitude toward others?
- What would it look like for you to honor sexual union in new ways?
- What keeps you from viewing sexual union as a spiritual bonding?

CHAPTER 7

Masturbation

If the heart is not naked along with the body, then the whole action becomes a lie and a mockery.
Mike Mason
The Mystery of Marriage

Question #5:

Is masturbation a sin?

So Much History, but Is It All Correct?

While I consider singleness to be the most overlooked aspect of sexuality, I believe the topic of masturbation holds the distinction of being the heaviest and most shame filled. As I listen to people's real questions about their sexuality, married and single, it saddens me to see this topic hold many, many of us captive to a very silent and paralyzing shame.

While we were talking about the joys and struggles of life over coffee one day, a single friend of mine haltingly shared that her journey with God continues to get hijacked by, "a nagging sin that is like a thorn in my side."

"Is it masturbation?" I asked.

The words were out of my mouth before I could retrieve them or temper them. Her horrified face, stunned silence, and crimson blush said it all: masturbation was the thorn that held her captive, and the shame was visible and vulnerable.

Is masturbation a sin?

The power of both this question and the pain-filled faces that have asked it have compelled me to dive deeper, beyond the myths and my own assumptions, into the folds of scripture in search of real hope and healing truth. Could God possibly help us reconcile the beauty of our sexuality with the seemingly destructive role that this shame-filled question has on people's lives?

In our quest for answers and Godly insight, we must first demystify and dispel the many myths about masturbation, for there's an unfortunate amount of misinformation around this topic.

How in the world did we get here?

"Masturbation" is defined by *Webster's Dictionary* as, "the stimulation of one's own genitals for sexual pleasure." The word has Latin roots: *manual* (hand) + *stupere* (to be stunned or stupefied).[125]

Masturbation is certainly not a new thing, though the language around it has evolved and changed dramatically through the years. Self-stimulation is portrayed in ancient art, dating back to at least the second century, and is often portrayed as a symbol of power and authority. The Egyptians celebrated self-stimulation as a testament to the power of life.

But masturbation has both a longstanding and storied history! Consider just some of the happenings and hang-ups around this topic in more recent history:

- *1340*—The word "pollution" originates as a reference to "discharge of semen other than during sex."[126]

---

125 *Online Etymology Dictionary.* Web. www.etymonline.com
126 *Online Dictionary.* Web. www.dictionary.com

- *1700s*—The Christian community uses "onanism" (more on this follows) as a reference to masturbation.
- 1760—Dr. Samuel Tissot, Swiss physician, claims masturbation is the "principal cause of mental illness" and became standard in all medical textbooks.[127]
- *1800s*—The washcloth is developed during the Victorian era for the purpose of preventing direct touching of the genitals during bathing.
- *1834*—Dr. Sylvester Graham, who considered masturbation to be especially harmful, created the graham cracker to reduce sexual cravings.[128]
- *1856–1932*—The U.S. Patent Office awards thirty-three patents to anti-masturbation devices, fourteen for humans.
- *1857*—The first recorded use of masturbate, a verb.
- *1884*—Dr. John Harvey Kellogg creates cornflakes to help curtail children's inclinations toward masturbation. [129]

There's quite the lore around masturbation, wouldn't you say?

Frankly, while much of this sounds very backward and archaic, misinformation about masturbation is perpetuated and rampant even today. Here are some present-day myths used in an attempt to squelch self-stimulation tendencies:

- The palm of your hand will grow hair.[130]
- Your penis could fall off.
- Masturbating causes bladder infections.
- Your heart will stop, and you can die from it.[131]
- Masturbation causes infertility.

---

127 Dolphin, Lambert. "Masturbation and The Bible." (2000): 20. [online.]
128 McLaren, Carrie. "Porn Flakes: Kellogg, Graham and the Crusade for Moral Fiber. Weblog post. *Stayfree Magazine*. www.stayfree.org
129 McLaren, Carrie. "Porn Flakes: Kellogg, Graham and the Crusade for Moral Fiber. Weblog post. *Stayfree Magazine*. www.stayfree.org]
130 Most of the world would be wearing gloves.
131 Actually, orgasm can cause the heart to race to the point of perhaps skipping a beat, but it actually can strengthen the heart muscle.

Recently, some teen boys asked me to confirm the truth of the first two mentioned—hairy palms and their penises falling off. Just the week prior, a priest had asserted these as fact in the boys' parochial school sex-education class.

While we might find these ideas laughable and absurd, they reflect what is often real discomfort with our genitals and shame-filled foundational beliefs about our own sexuality. Using unhealthy fear as a deterrent leads to shame, and shame typically leads to hiding. In fact, the Bible attests that hiding is the earliest recorded response to shame. In Genesis 3:8, the man and woman respond to their shame by hiding their bodies from one another and then from God. By avoiding truth and talk on this subject, we risk sending people into shame and hiding.

Most first introductions to self-stimulation happen in young children, who simply stumble upon their genitals as a natural part of exploring their own bodies. God created us with natural curiosity and a desire to explore the world around us; naturally, we explore and examine our bodies. Just watch small children's utter amazement at discovering their own hands and feet. The human body was designed to respond to physical touch, so imagine (or even remember yourself) the wonder of a young child discovering his or her own genitals!

Now, imagine this discovery in the context of cause and effect. When my daughter was eighteen months old, she flipped the light switch eighty-seven times (that I counted). She reveled in the cause/effect dynamic: switch—light, switch—dark, switch—light, switch—dark. Over and over again, she clearly enjoyed this pattern as part of her natural curiosity and discovery process.

Do you have an early memory of the pleasurable sensation that resulted from stimulating your genitals? What emotions attached to this experience: shame, joy, comfort, fear?

I remember another day as a mother, when one of my daughters came running naked from the bathroom with a handheld mirror. She had just discovered, to her utter amazement, that she had three holes in "her privates." I remember feeling frozen in time as I chose whether to respond out of my shock and, frankly, embarrassment, or to respond in an honest, straightforward way to her natural curiosity.

So, if curiosity about our genitals and self-stimulation happen early and are natural parts of our curiosity, it's imperative that we learn and find language to speak the truth about masturbation. Are we willing to examine this topic with the purpose of true understanding and bringing life?

What Scripture Says on the Subject

Frankly, the concept of self-stimulation, let alone the literal word "masturbation," is nowhere to be found in scripture.

However, some in the Christian community would beg to differ, based on a common interpretation of the story of Onan, as found in Genesis 38:1–10. In this scripture, God struck Onan dead as a result of his, "wasting his seed on the ground." But, if we examine this scripture closely, is it really a death sentence for Onan's self-stimulation or something altogether different?

In this scriptural account, Onan's brother has died, leaving Onan's sister-in-law a widow. The God-ordained provision for protecting and providing for widowed women within the Jewish culture required that Onan lay with his sister-in-law, "to perform his duty as a brother-in-law ... and raise up offspring," for his brother.[132] In this way, his brother's name would be carried forward, and Onan's widowed sister-in-law would be provided for as a part of an ongoing family. But, when Onan's father sent him into his brother's tent, Onan entered but then spilled his seed on the ground and was later struck dead as a result.

While some have interpreted that God took Onan's life as a result of his "masturbation," the passage clearly states that Onan lost his life as a result of his own defiance and greedy desire to claim a greater

---

132 Genesis 38:8.

inheritance, which would have been compromised by additional offspring. Besides this, we know that Onan was not in the tent alone, and more than likely, he used his sister-in-law for his pleasure and chose to withdraw before "fulfilling his duty." [133]

So, if scripture is silent on the topic of masturbation, where does that leave us? It would be easy to jump into one of two camps by default:

- *Scripture is silent*, so masturbation must be okay; God would have said something if it was wrong.
- *Scripture is cryptic,* but if we read between the lines, we can see how wrong it is and what God really meant.

In either of these, what is our true motivation? Are we more interested in justifying our preferred way of thinking or in defaulting to black-and-white thinking?

We must never take scripture's *omission* as *permission*. Many things are not dealt with specifically in scripture—cocaine, for example—but God gave us the ability to discern and make healthy choices. And where we'd like easily prescribed answers, God invites us instead to live a life in active dialogue and discernment.

While scripture doesn't address masturbation outright, it repeatedly speaks to issues of self-control and the powerful lure of lust. So, the bigger question here might be, who is in control—you or the act of masturbation?

But before we go there, let's look to a couple other points that can help inform our thinking and discernment on this topic. Specifically,

- What does God's intentional design of our body have to lend to this discussion?
- Are singles excluded from the amazing health benefits that orgasm offers?
- What role does self-care have in masturbation?

---

133 The correct term for this is "coitus interruptus," when a man withdraws from a woman's vagina before ejaculating.

What does God's intentional design of our body have to lend to this discussion?

God did not design us to settle for imitations of pleasure but, instead, to experience the ultimate wonder of our physical design. Our bodies were designed to experience pleasure, thus the numerous nerve endings that pack the male and female genitals.

When I was in sixth grade, all students were required to complete various physical challenges as a part of the President's Physical Fitness Program. One of those challenges was using our own strength to climb a rope to the top of the gym to ring a bell. While climbing the rope, I experienced a wonderful sensation that left me feeling like I could fly! I lingered at the top of the rope at these moments, unaware of anything around me. During my three years in middle school, Mrs. Bates would always pick me to demonstrate this exercise to the new students. Honestly, I had no idea why everyone didn't love climbing the rope! I remember asking my friend if she experienced "this thing" with the rope, and she had no idea what I meant.[134] I interpreted her response to mean that "this pleasure" I could not explain was inappropriate and there clearly was something wrong with me for feeling it. I felt shame.

There are so many parts of our body that were designed to give us pleasure, yet *none of them were designed to give us life in and of themselves.* God's hand designed man and woman's physical bodies, and declared that how we are made is "very good."[135] I do not have the authority or the power to proclaim as shameful that which was proclaimed as "very good." The true essence of our design has something to teach us about who God is. Our body's ability to experience pleasure through a variety of means is part of learning discernment in how we view masturbation.

Are singles excluded from the amazing health benefits that orgasm offers?

---

134 I later learned it was an orgasm.
135 Genesis 1:31.

While masturbation does not offer the same level of hormonal release as intercourse, it can definitely offer health benefits. Orgasm, by its very nature, is a total body engagement, not just a pelvic event. Nerve endings are stimulated, chemicals surge through the brain, and muscles throughout the body contract and release. Orgasm is a deep mind and body interchange.

Here are just some of the whole-health benefits that orgasm offers.

- *Boosts testosterone and estrogen in both men and women.* Some physicians suggest that testosterone keeps hearts healthy and good cholesterol high. The estrogen released during orgasm helps promote vaginal elasticity.
- *Increases blood flow.* Accelerated heart rate and deep breathing increase the blood flow to all the body's organs, cells, and muscles. This helps reduce stress and promotes relaxation, and it helps reduce women's abdominal cramping during periods.
- *Reduces pain.* "In a study published in the *Bulletin of Experimental Biology and Medicine*, forty-eight volunteers who inhaled oxytocin vapor and then had their fingers pricked lowered their pain threshold by more than half."[136]
- *Increases pelvic floor muscle control for women.* Orgasms help strengthen this often undervalued part of a woman's body. Exercising the pelvic muscles with regular Kegel exercises will help to minimize the risk of incontinence later in life.[137]
- *Reduces risk of prostate cancer.* In men, frequent ejaculations have been proven to lower the risk of prostate cancer later in life.[138]

---

136 Doherty, Kathleen. "10 Surprising Health Benefits of Sex." Web MD – Better Information. Better Health. 2008.Web. www.webmd.com

137 Tighten the muscles of your pelvic floor (as if you want to stop the flow of urine) count to three, and release. Repeat seven to ten times, three times each day, for two weeks to begin noticing a difference. This can also be practiced during intercourse.

138 Doherty, Kathleen. "10 Surprising Health Benefits of Sex." Web MD – Better Information. Better Health. 2008.Web. www.webmd.com.

When I speak on the health benefits of orgasm in my classes, singles typically ask, "Would God want to exclude me from these because I am single?"

That is a very good question, one that begs us to consider again how we view God, our sexual drive, and ourselves.

What role does self-care have in masturbation?

When we know our body and its natural rhythm and desires, we have the opportunity to care for our body in a "whole-istic" way, honoring both how God has made us and desires for us to experience our sexuality in holy and healthy ways.

These stories and others have helped inform and expand my view of masturbation as a potential form of self-care.

- A man who travels a great deal shared with me that he chooses to "take his wife with him" on his trips by calling her to have "phone sex." This has served as a sacred connection for them and has expanded their ability both to communicate through words and care for one another physically in the long absences that strain their bodies.
- While speaking at a conference, I met a woman who had just said good-bye to her husband for a year's deployment in Iraq. Together, they had made a covenant to guard their relationship emotionally and physically. These two were intentional in discussing the challenges they would face and how best to care for their respective sexual needs. They made "connection covenants" for their relationship and their bodies—using visual memories to come present to one another and self-stimulate—and were then intentional to share their experiences with each other when they talked across the miles.
- A man I know was at the doctor's office to give a sperm sample. He was sent into a room to find walls lined with pornographic material, something he had been

addicted to in years past. As he attempted to "spill his seed," he realized he found no pleasure in the images and would need to switch rooms. When he moved to another room, he found that he needed no images to complete the task; God was with him, and stimulating his genitals became a sacred act.

Where does this information lead us in our quest around the topic of masturbation?

If we see our bodies as designed by God with purpose and believe that every part of our body is meant to bring glory to God, then yes, I believe there are appropriate places and times to engage with our body and share the pleasure with God. But if we separate our sexuality from our spirituality, we settle for a cheap imitation of the richness God intended.

Sex was never designed to be self-focused. It was designed to be a deeper pull into an intimate relationship with God and with a spouse in marriage. Its truest nature is to strengthen a spirit, mind, and body connection. We have a choice to view our genitals and sexual urges through one of two lenses:

- Self-gratification—I need it, I want it, and I am entitled to it.
- Soul-gratification—Experiencing our bodies in partnership with God

Masturbation can be about consuming something for a moment's pleasure, something we allow to be beyond our control. It can be a force that demands to be separate and independent from what God designed as whole and holy—spirit, mind, and body. Or, it can be a place of lingering with God as the ultimate Designer. It can help us partner with God in addressing our body's desires in healthy ways.

"Anything that rubs peoples' noses in their mortality is also capable of lifting their hearts to God."[139] Through the Spirit of God, we can

---

139 Mason, Mike. *Mystery of Marriage*. Sisters: Multnomah, 1985. p. 148. Print.

experience the full integration of our mind and body—a wholeness that is holy sexuality at the core.

How might God meet me, and what might my body have to teach me about God?

An Important Distinction: Self-Exploration

There are important distinctions to be made in this discussion of self-stimulation, not just about the possibility of self-care, but also about the potential benefits of self-exploration. The opportunity to know our own body better can both expand our relationship with God our Creator and expand our partnership and intimacy with our spouse. And there are important differences here between men and women.

Men are well acquainted with their bodies and genitals as a natural part of everyday life, as they experience elimination and sexual arousal through their penises. This part of their body is very obvious and, frankly, hands-on. And, as a powerhouse of pleasure, it yields a very predictable response to stimulation.

It can be easy for both men and women to fall into the trap of thinking that women's awareness of their genitals, their arousal-ability, and sense of pleasure should be just as matter of fact. Nothing could be further from the truth.

Women's genitals are far more mysterious and hidden. Unlike men's genitals, which are practical daily companions, women's are more akin to a distant third cousin once removed!

The woman's power-packed clitoris is tucked inside her body, hidden from view. The only way to "see" and understand this area is through touch—or self-exploration. Not only that, but each woman's body is unique in terms of things like elasticity, responses to pressure, the tipping of the uterus, and so on, and no two clitorises are the same, so each woman's means of arousal is incredibly unique to her.

Self-exploration becomes a means of knowing one's own body in order to understand the sacred treasure of how our body is designed. For women, it is too often assumed that men know how to pleasure women and satisfy sexual desires. Yet, men know and perceive sex through their own experiences and cannot be responsible to know fully the complexities of women's pleasure potential. Exploring our own body allows women to partner with their spouses, guide men in what gives pleasure, and make sex a more mutual, less one-sided experience.

How might self-exploration enrich our understanding of God's one-of-a-kind design of our body? How might it enrich our relationship with our spouse?

The Heart of the Matter: Motives and Red Flags

If we respect the design of our sexual organs and honor the Creator of our bodies, we will consider our heart's motive for engaging with our genitals, the habits we have created, and how vulnerable we are with God. If you find that self-care or exploration is leading you toward any of these thoughts or patterns, it's time to pause and ask who is really in control.

- *Isolation*— when we seek a physical high at the expense of relationships—with God or others
- *Disassociation*—when we separate the spiritual and emotional from the physical act of masturbation and aren't living integrated with our genitals and personal sexual desires
- *Uncontrollable habit*—when self-stimulation is a driving force or our mind-set is, "My sexual drive has a mind of its own, and I cannot control it"
- *Dependency*—when we become dependent on the sexual release as a necessary part of the day, to clear our mind, or reduce stress
- *Habitual avoidance*—when self-stimulation serves as a means of disengaging from a relationship, challenging

situations, or as justification for "not bothering my spouse"

- *Pornography*—when we use visual images as a means of fantasy or stimulation, which is proven to create neural pathways in our brain that lead, over time, to us seeing men and women only as potential porn stars[140]

If we know the power of such intense pleasure, it is important that we also know the potential danger it holds.

It had been almost a year since the surprising and vulnerable conversation between my shocked friend and I, in which I suggested that she consider if and how God might meet her in what she considered to be this "nagging sin." She now spoke of a freedom that she was experiencing in her sexuality. She displayed a radiance that echoed of life.

As she began to recognize her use of masturbation as an escape from feeling past and present pain, her compulsion became her awareness that she was hiding from God. As she began to come present, asking God to guide her in a new way, she began to experience an active desire to bring her physical and emotional needs to God. She remarked that what had once been addictive and isolating was gradually becoming a sacred place of connection and no longer a physical escape from God. Instead of a compulsive response, she was living with an awareness of her spirit and body that engaged her mind. She was no longer captive and without control.

The invitation is before us in the sacred words that were spoken to Moses and chiseled into stone, "You shall have no other gods before me."[141] These are not words of command but words of life offered to help us protect the potential of our relationship with God. From within the Garden, we see the pursuit of God in how we were formed and fashioned to be in a face-to-face relationship with our Creator.

---

140 There is a vast amount of research that is currently being done on how pornography hijacks the brain's ability to develop intimacy. *Wired for Intimacy*, by William M. Struthers is an excellent resource.

141 Genesis 20:3.

In studying with a rabbi, he invited me to look anew at these ancient words from within the Hebrew heritage. We see the Ten Commandments and translate them as if from a dictator laying down the rules. Yet, in Hebrew, the text reads only as *Ten Words*. God gave these words to bring life and foster a face-to-face relationship with God as an ongoing reality rather than an exception.

This brave woman so eloquently illustrates this true meaning of the first word that was given in that she *stripped down the gods* of fear, shame, and pain that she had built up between her and her Creator. From the vantage point of being able to see more clearly, she risked trusting that God wanted to be face-to-face *with her*. She chose to have, "no other gods in God's face."

The deepest invitation in knowing one's body is the intimate, face-to-face gaze of our Creator.

Some Questions for Reflection

- How might God want to meet you, and what might your physical body have to teach you?
- Have you personally experienced fear and shame around masturbation?
- What does God's invitation seem to be for you around this topic?
- What would it look like to discern and dialogue with God about your body?
- If there are new thoughts that this information raises, what might God be saying to you personally on this topic?

CHAPTER 8

To Be Continued ...

Bidden or unbidden, God is present.
Spartan Proverb

God Pursues Us

A number of years ago, a dear friend of mine was diagnosed with cancer. When she shared the news with her children, her small son became incredibly upset and ran from the house. Instinctively, I ran after him, wrestled him to the ground, and held him in a vice grip as his pain oozed out through sobs, screams, and kicks. I don't remember uttering any words that day, but I do remember a sense of divine strength that came through me as I held this flailing child close to my heart. I had a deep desire to walk in and through all the unknowns and questions and struggles with this precious boy.

As I held him tightly and began to rock back and forth, there was a point at which he ceased to fight me and allowed me to just hold him. His body finally relaxed, and he melted deep into my chest with a pain-filled cascade of tears and breathless questions I could not answer. He gradually eased into rhythmic, deep, peaceful breathing. This young boy wanted answers that were easy and safe. No one could change the reality that cancer would take his mother's life. He would have to walk this journey, but he was not alone.

When I think of sexuality and spirituality and how we so often have segregated the two, I am reminded of the experience of holding fiercely to this child. For many of us, inviting God into this seemingly "private part" of our life can feel threatening and overwhelming, but where we might want to run in the opposite direction, God is the one pursuing us and longing to hold us and walk with us.

Questions become the gateway through which we tread upon this "new-ancient"[142] territory of our body's intentional design. That God took the time to initiate an intimate relationship with each gender in the process of forming and fashioning them indicates the great intentionality with which the Creator moved toward the created.

Do we see our sexuality as very good?

Can we see with the eyes of our Creator the potential for life that is embedded within one another?

Heart-Aching Questions

Truth will always withstand the scrutiny of examination, and never has there been a more relevant time than now to wonder and examine the truest essence of our sexual design. I am reminded of this by the numbers of married and single people who dare to share their heart-aching questions and longings with me while seeking to understand their sexuality in deeper ways by:

- Struggling to remember with how many people they have shared their body
- Acknowledging gnawing feelings of guilt the morning after
- Wondering if this really is all there is
- Realizing that they no longer feel attracted to a spouse
- Wrestling with the idea of making love to the same person for the rest of their life
- Wondering if sex could hold more than just momentary pleasure

---

142 A statement that I have heard J. Philip Newell use when teaching about Scripture's ancient truths that continue to reveal the absolute wonder of God in new ways.

Might the questions be the windows through which we discover something more? Could our longings be a pathway through which we discover more of who God is and what resources our Creator has provided for our good?

Continuing On

While the mystery continues to unfold and be revealed in this day and age, there are foundational truths that can reveal the genuine beauty of our sexuality and release us from settling for a cheap imitation.

Holy Sexuality is:

- Being mindful of my own gender and the gender of others
- Respecting and valuing differences of men and women as part of God's design
- Living alive to the sensuousness of spirit, mind, and body
- Trusting that the true root of my sexual desire is from God's abundant love
- Inviting God to be a sacred partner in sexual union

Embracing our sexuality is a journey, a place of ongoing discovery, a means of holding the beauty of how we are made, and engaging with the One who created us.

My friend's battle with cancer ended recently. At her funeral, her now-grown son—without an ounce of struggle—surrendered his head and flowing tears against my chest. With moist eyes and a choked voice, he shared that his mother's cancer had taught him to treasure deeply each moment of life. He had held the beauty of life amid the threat of death. Joy and pain had intermingled in the years between, but ultimately, he had let the journey tutor him. His questions and struggles were his guide, and he continues to walk through them all with others who continue to walk with him.

By facing the questions head-on, this fine young man has experienced the reality of these sacred words that David, the psalmist, penned:

> Open your mouth and taste, open your eyes and
> see—Blessed are you who run to Him![143]

Does the potential of all that our sexuality holds cause us to run to God or away from God?

I once heard Philip Newell say, "Christ didn't come to show us who we weren't; He came to show us what we are humanly capable of." When we truly know who we are, we see how our lives are interwoven with others. We see value in those things others might overlook. We find the mystery of God's love both dangerous and inviting. Freedom comes in living within this mystery rather than letting comfort, fear, and conclusions dictate how we live.

As I examine Jesus' life, I see Him living abundantly free within the questions. Though the cross was not a desire, make no mistake that Jesus committed to it from a freedom of knowing who He was by recognizing the abundant love of God. Jesus embraced the strength of the love that sustained Him. It was not nails that held that body to the cross: it was love, a love so deep, so rich, and so abundant it held the truest essence of a full identity found within God.

As human beings, we seek closure and long to have things wrapped up in a neat package, with all the answers clear and finalized. We like to believe that answers will be our quest's reward and that lingering questions are a sign that we didn't do our job.

When my crumbling foundational beliefs no longer held up to the storms in my life, real-life questions became my guide and led my journey into the depths of sexuality, which revealed the interwoven threads of spirituality. Pain and poor choices littered my past, but I discovered they did not need to define my future. Although I've learned much and have had a deep desire to share what has been written here, my quest continues. Rather than always finding hard and fast answers, I have found Someone who walks with me, loves to hold me, engages in ongoing dialogues, and journeys forward *with me*. God continues to teach me as "we" engage in exploring

---

143 Psalms 34:8.

my sexuality, which bears the fingerprints of God and is designed to reflect this sacred image within the world.

God has called me to live life with abundance and joy, and I know no better way than through living in the fullness of my truest identity without shame or fear. An Estonian proverb says it this way, "The work will teach you how to do it." My desire is to invite you into the work, to continue on this journey of examination, trusting that the questions will continue to inform and guide you. God knows the way of returning to the Garden, and an invitation is extended to you to remember.

Once again, a question arises: how might the truth of sexuality and spirituality as God's design release and reclaim God's love within us?

And ...

How might living out that love impact the world around us?

Appendix A

Some Guidelines of Holy Sexuality for Singles

Engage the mind: Our brain must be actively engaged with our sexuality.

- Our brain is the largest sex organ in the body. Stress is felt first in the genitals in the form of a tingling sensation.[144] Our brain has a sexual brake that can literally pull the blood back from the genital region.
- Engage in conversation with a trusted friend about what you're facing; don't isolate yourself.
- Dialogue with your dating partner is both required and enriching. Don't assume another knows what you're thinking or what your specific goals and values are around sex.

Listen to your own body: Sex drives are unique to the individual.

- Genital blood flow increases when we're attracted to someone.
- Clothing friction to the genitals can cause vulnerability.

---

144 This is easy to see in small boys when they experience stress or a new situation; they immediately reach down and touch themselves. Because girls genitals are more secluded, often they will reference their stress as a stomach ache.

- Women have a libido spike in the middle of their monthly cycle.
- A twenty-second meaningful touch can release oxytocin—a bonding chemical—into a woman's bloodstream.
- Recognize if/when sexual release could be a helpful form of self-care.[145]
- Vigorous physical activity helps release sexual energy.

Recognize your triggers: These, too, are unique to each person.

- Recognize what you find attractive in terms of a person's body, how they think, and how they spiritually engage.
- Scent is the most underestimated sexual turn-on.
- Location, location, location; when feeling vulnerable, be careful in what situations you place yourself.
- Couples who learn to engage in conversation aren't as quick to move to sexual activity.
- Romantic novels and movies can trigger physical/emotional longings.
- What we watch can fuel feelings; pornography comes in all forms—primetime TV, music videos, and so on.

Take responsibility: Identify your own values around sex.

- Dig deep, and identify your own goals about sex; others' prescribed goals don't tend to stick in the heat of the battle.
- Don't abdicate responsibility and expect your partner to be your conscience.
- Isolation when dating is dangerous; community is required.
- Ask a trusted friend for accountability around your sexual boundaries. Speaking our feelings out loud can help diminish their power over us.
- Value and honor the other gender, being sensitive to their challenges and vulnerabilities.

---

145 See chapter 7.

Appendix B

Soul Ties Prayer

Dear God,

I acknowledge you as the Creator of my spirit, mind, and body. The mystery of how you have designed the intimate intricacy of this is beyond my understanding. I choose to recognize and submit to the beauty of your original design within me.

I ask your forgiveness for the ways I have partnered my spirit, mind, and body with others. I acknowledge that I am choosing to reclaim what you designed as "very good" by your own hand.

I release within me all remnants of others that I have received into my being through emotional, sexual, or spiritual exchange. I ask you to gather these parts from within me and return them to the their place of origin within another.

As these places within me are severed, I ask that you would hold each vulnerable part of my inner most being. Prepare my deepest design—spiritually, emotionally, and physically—to receive back all elements of my truest identity and how these sacred places are to be held within me.

I call to those parts of myself that have been taken away or that I have given to others—spiritually, emotionally, or physically. I invite you to return to the intended resting place that is within me and that holds the truest design of God as the Creator of my spirit, mind, and body.

I ask that you, the Designer of the most intimate places within me, rejoin and restore:

> my mind to hold the truth of your loving power ...

> my body to reclaim the fullness of my physical design ...

> my spirit to embrace the image I hold of You ...

I invite the fullness of your intentional "good" of my spirit, mind, and body to be joined together completely and fully for the purpose of living abundantly within you. What you have joined together, I claim as whole and declare that no man can separate.

Amen.

A note to the reader:

This is not a magic formula but a guideline that I submit for you as a resource. If you are feeling called toward this, I recommend taking the time to notice the names, faces, and situations that arise within your thinking. Write them down, record your thoughts, images and choose to see them outside of yourself. This becomes the "physical" evidence that you can symbolically destroy.

We are not meant to walk through life in isolation. I have found that inviting a trusted friend, counselor, or pastor to walk through this with you holds significance to how you continue to walk this out. Pray about who it is that you would see as a partner to continue to remind you of the future not being dictated by the past.

May you experience the freedom of who you truly are within the loving design of bearing the image of our Creator.

God is crazy about you!

~becky

Natalie Patton Photography ©2010

Becky Patton is the founder and owner of Truessence—a business/ ministry committed to informing and enriching lives, and responding to real-life questions with a hope-filled message of God's true design for sexuality and spirituality. She speaks first-hand of finding powerful, practical hope in seemingly hopeless circumstances, including the debilitating pain of sexual abuse and the cascading impact this brought into marriage. She is a pastor and speaker, with a message relevant to women, men, married and single.

Becky is a wife of 30+ years, mother of two grown daughters, a pastor, and a speaker—but at her core, she is a curious and complex woman created by the loving hand of God...that mysteriously also craves barbecued potato chips and dark chocolate in mass quantities. Find out more at www.truessence.net